ABOUT

Ninad Karpe h
starting with being a consultant, moving on to
a corporate job in a global multinational and
eventually to an Indian listed company, as a
Board member.

Today, Karpe is a strategy consultant, working
across different corporates and mentors
Indian companies to make a mark on the
global stage.

He is the Chairman of the Western Region of
the Confederation of Indian Industry (CII) for
2016-17, which is an honorary position. CII is
a non-government, not-for-profit, industry-led
and industry-managed organisation.

Karpe is a Director of Aptech Ltd. and was
the MD and CEO of the same company for
several years. During his seven year stint
as MD and CEO at Aptech, Karpe turned
around the company and expanded its
footprint to cover 42 emerging countries,
with its brands of Arena and Aptech.

He previously served CA Technologies, the
world's fourth largest software vendor as MD,
covering India and SAARC countries, where
he was associated with the company for more
than 13 years, since its inception in India.

Earlier in his career, Karpe worked as a
consultant, advising companies seeking
to invest in India. He frequently writes for

magazines and contributes to management schools by presentations on marketing and business strategy.

Karpe serves as an independent director on the boards of a number of public companies – IDBI Bank, BNP Paribas AMC, EDC Ltd, NSE Academy Ltd and Savita Oil Technologies Ltd. He also mentors SLONKIT, a fintech start-up and has joined the Board of SK Restaurants, promoted by celebrity Chef Sanjeev Kapoor to guide them in expanding operations outside India.

During the F1 season, Karpe switches off his mobile phone on race day and seriously follows the fast-paced cars on the circuit. He has a rare but interesting hobby of home wine-making and spends considerable time in understanding the taste as well as business of wines.

Karpe is married and lives in Mumbai with his wife, who is a teacher. His elder son got married recently and works in the US and his younger son is pursuing his undergraduate studies.

PRAISE FOR THE BOOK

"Business strategies are crucial to the growth of any company and are also significant in any investment decision. Ninad's book is a must-have for the lessons it pulls out from a range of events that help towards defining and implementing business strategies."

Rakesh Jhujhunwala
Ace Investor

"The latest insights into strategy and management come from using a completely different set of lenses. I am delighted to see the creative approach Ninad Karpe has used - drawing on such diverse contemporary phenomena as pro Kabaddi, Hardik Patel and *Baahubali* - to give us a new way of looking at management in today's complex and rapidly changing world."

Prof. Rishi Krishnan
Director and Professor
of Strategy, IIM, Indore

"Ninad's sharp eyes and innovative mind cull nuggets of business strategy wisdom by studying domains unconventional to present business studies. His examples include Kejriwal to James Bond, F1 race to Kabaddi and many other new sources. A must for business executives, academia and business students to widen strategy perspective."

Ashank Desai
Founder of Mastek
Founder member and
ex-Chairman, NASSCOM

"*Bond to Baba* is a fascinating book on the practice of strategy and the many real life illustrations make it an interesting read for management professionals and students."

C. Y. Pal
Corporate Leader
ex-Chairman, Cadbury India

"Ninad with his years of hand on experience of creating and implementing strategy has put together an immensely readable and insightful book on abstracting the key elements of a successful strategy. Practical and useful, this is a highly recommended read for any practitioners of modern management."

Bharat Puri
Managing Director
Pidilite Industries Ltd

"Taking cues from current and historical topics across entertainment, sports, politics and business, Ninad brings in a fresh perspective to the concept of 'strategy' in *Bond to Baba*. He delves deep and beautifully analyzes each 'use case', elucidating different practical applications of strategy. Ninad's neoteric approach shrouds the existing Agile and LEAN schools of thought and lends a realistic direction to go-to-market strategies, pivoting on crucial timelines."

Keshav R. Murugesh
Group CEO
- WNS Global Services

Warm regards...

Ninad.
2018

BOND
to
BABA

#SuccessfulStrategies

Ninad Karpe

PopulaR
prakashan
www.popularprakashan.com

Published by Harsha Bhatkal
for Popular Prakashan Pvt. Ltd.
301, Mahalaxmi Chambers
22, Bhulabhai Desai Road
Mumbai - 400026
www.popularprakashan.com

(4491)
ISBN 978-81-7991-932-3

Design: Gopi Kukde

Printed by
by Saurabh Printers (P) Ltd.
Plot No. 67 A-68, Ecotech, Ext. I
Kasna, Greater Noida-201306 (U.P)

This book is dedicated to

My father,

B. S. Karpe

21 March, 1927 to 28 February, 2010

Remembering you, every day!

CONTENTS

FOREWORD

Bond to Baba is a highly personal take on strategy that is simultaneously entertaining and insightful. Ninad ranges wide in his examples, drawing on Hollywood and Bollywood, MNC and Indian firm marketing, and Kabbadi, cricket-captaincy and Formula 1 to illustrate his principles of strategy. You may not share all of Ninad's enthusiasms, but we can learn from particularly the unfamiliar. I share his love for James Bond movies but I learnt more from digesting why *Baahubali* and *Sairat* should be quite so popular. By the end of the book, I came away with some core principles of strategy nicely reinforced.

To me, strategy starts with choice. Choice is not only about what one should do, but what one should not do. By focusing on a niche, such as a regional appeal, a low-budget film like *Sairat* can be hugely successful and Wagh Bakri can enter a market dominated by global brands at the top end and generics at the mass end. Staying true to the choice one makes, and developing a back-end that is appropriate to the choices one has made delivers enduring value.

Second, strategy needs to be constantly refreshed. The reinvention of what is cool about James Bond may gall some of us purists, but it

keeps people watching by the million.
An initial formula maybe very successful,
but unless one keeps up with changing taste
one could end up like HMT, with a long,
lingering death.

Third, if one is successful one should know
why. The examples of Hardik Patel and
Arvind Kejriwal are telling – the powerful
appeal of a simple message can be
muddied by inconsistency in performance
or a lack of follow-through to build on
initial achievement.

And finally, good strategy can be trumped
by better execution. Adaptation, nimbleness,
constant tweaking and improving can deliver
the sustained results that outclass those with
a headstart and greater resources.

But I'm keeping you from both Bond and
Baba, so on with the show.

— **Dr Naushad Forbes**
Co-Chairman, Forbes Marshall
and Immediate Past President,
Confederation of Indian Industry (CII)

PREFACE

"Another book on Strategy?!" My friends seemed visibly shocked when I announced my plan to write a book on this subject. The only reason I persisted with my plan was because of a quiet conviction that this book on strategy would be uniquely different.

For the past decade or so, I have been regularly writing in a leading Indian business magazine, on various business topics, including strategy. While writing an article requires effort, writing a book entails an entirely different level of depth, diligence and dedication.

From what was mistakenly envisaged as a low intensity effort of two months to write this book, I finally took more than twelve months of steady effort, sweat and toil. At the end of it, deeper introspection led to the creation of new ideas and thoughts, finally culminating into this book!

With strategies ranging from reinvention of a business to resurrection and brand extension — the book explores the serious aspects of strategy with real-life analogies, like the reinvention of the character of James Bond in *Skyfall*, the success of the Pro Kabaddi League and the phenomenal commercial

success of Patanjali products promoted by
Baba Ramdev.

Finally, you can read this book as a good
story and a narration of these various
examples or attempt an in-depth analysis
of the strategy outlined in each chapter and
apply it to your real-life situation.

I must thank my ex-colleague, Shrutidhar
Paliwal, for cajoling me into getting started
with this book. My family – my wife Anjali
and my sons Saahil and Neel – have always
supported and encouraged my writing, ever
willing to give me critical feedback. My
younger son Neel, passed judgement on
the first draft and his feedback was crisp
and immediate.

My wife Anjali, has always been my greatest
strength, my harshest critic and my in-house
editor –. she painstakingly went through the
manuscript, making it look far better than
the original.

My heartfelt thanks to Dr Naushad Forbes,
Co-Chairman, Forbes Marshall and
Immediate Past President, Confederation of
Indian Industry (CII), for embellishing this
book by writing a foreword. Gopi Kukde,
the celebrated Adman has done an amazing
job in designing the cover and the inside of
this book – using several conversations to
understand the heart of the book.

Without the efforts of Vinayak Gawande,
Harsha Bhatkal and their team at

Popular Prakashan, this book would not have seen the light of its day – a special thanks to them for believing in the book and all that it had to offer.

I have certainly enjoyed writing this book. Now go ahead and read it! Like it? Or hate it? Let me know…

— Ninad Karpe
bondtobaba@gmail.com
#BondtoBaba
ninad-karpe
@NinadKarpe
@BondtoBaba

BOND AND THE ART OF REINVENTION

No individual or business can remain static, especially in these times of rapid change. To remain relevant and contemporary, it is important to reinvent at periodic intervals – not just change for the sake of change, but for reinventing the core. By its nature, the reinvention of a business requires courage and boldness. If such reinvention is done in a thoughtful manner, the chances of it succeeding are high. There is a massive pile of management literature on this topic. It is extensive and pretty thorough. Yet, this piece of writing looks at the subject anew – deriving lessons by focusing the lens on the James Bond franchise. Reinventing itself over time, the James Bond franchise remains popular as ever and as relevant after more than 55 years.

Ian Fleming was the creator of the character of James Bond. During the Second World War he worked for the Naval Intelligence and once the war was over, he settled in Jamaica in a bungalow that he called *Goldeneye*, after a wartime operation in which he was involved. The fictional character of James Bond was created and Fleming wrote his first book, *Casino Royale*, which was published in 1952.

This book became a huge success and thus began the journey of James Bond. Combining his background of journalism and wartime service, Fleming envisioned Bond as an officer of MI6 the British Secret Intelligence service, with his code number as 007 and as a commander in the Royal Naval Reserve. After so many years, these aspects of the character of James Bond remain unchanged.

Dr. No was the first film of the Bond franchise and was released in 1962, although it was not the first novel written by Ian Fleming. Starring Sean Connery and Ursula Andress, it was made on a shoestring budget of $1 million. As against this, the cost of producing *Skyfall* in 2012 was around $200 million and *Spectre* was upwards of $300 million – the most expensive Bond film made. The iconic line, "The name's Bond...James Bond" was first used in *Dr. No* and became an instant rage. The Bond franchise has spilled over more than five decades and has been the most successful film franchise. Over the years numerous actors have essayed the role of James Bond.

To mark the 50th anniversary of the first Bond film, *Skyfall* was released in 2012 with Daniel Craig as James Bond. This was his third movie as Bond; the earlier two being *Casino Royale* released in 2006, followed by *Quantum of Solace*, which was released in 2008. *Skyfall* marked the beginning of the reinvention of James Bond.

As an example, in *Skyfall*, a young geeky Q played by Ben Whishaw, hands over two gadgets to James Bond – a gun, which works only with Bond's palms and a radio. And then Q passes a snide remark "Were you expecting an exploding pen? We don't really go in for that anymore!" In the many changes, which Bond fans had to deal with, this really sums up the reinvention of James Bond in *Skyfall*. Ben Whishaw at 31, is the youngest Q in a Bond film.

A Bond purist would argue that there was really no need to look at the Bond character afresh, given its huge success over the years.

So, why was this done? What was different in *Skyfall?* And does it hold any lessons for business and strategy?

Competition

James Bond was a unique spy. He was surrounded by gorgeous girls, drank bountifully, bedded women, drove fancy cars and visited exotic locales around the world. And then there came a new breed of agents – Jason Bourne in 2002 played by Matt Damon, a mysterious Black Ops CIA officer who was an expert in martial arts, firearms and explosives and fluent in many languages. Movies like *The Fast and the Furious and Mission Impossible* had stunts, which left the viewers gasping. Clearly, the Bond franchise needed a reboot. And the Oscar award-winning director Sam Mendes crafted the role of Bond differently in *Skyfall.* Played brilliantly by Daniel Craig, *Skyfall* had the normal trappings of a Bond movie. However, Daniel Craig not only dodged bullets and drove fast cars, but also had a tough physique and demonstrated a great combination of brawn and brain.

Competition for any business follows the same pattern. Maintaining a leadership position is never easy and to do that it is incumbent on the leader to constantly rethink, reinvent and reboot. Business leaders are continually faced with complex problems: constant technology changes, increasing competition, fight for good talent and so on. In such a volatile environment, a steady business performance is just not enough. It is imperative to constantly reinvent. IBM, for example, has reinvented itself from a computer hardware company to a company where it earns a major portion of its revenues from services.

Apple has been known as a company which constantly reinvents to stay ahead of competition. Many of its blockbuster products are not original inventions, but reinvented to give them mass consumer appeal which its competitors have failed to do.

After Steve Jobs came back to Apple in 1997 he navigated the company on the path of reinvention. As a start, he reinvented the Mac machine by introducing the candy-coloured iMacs. After this, there was a series of reinventions – the iPod revolutionised the way we listen to music, tablets were reinvented with the introduction of iPads, smartphones came in with the iPhone and watches changed with the iWatch. What next? Will it be a car? Irrespective of the product launched by Apple, reinvention is now part of the company's DNA – a useful lesson for other companies wanting to reinvent and stay ahead of the competition!

Emotional intelligence

In *Skyfall* Bond clearly displays emotions and even sheds tears in the climactic scene with M. In fact M is almost shown as a surrogate mother to his orphaned life. In another scene, when Silva flirts with Bond and fondles his shirt collar, there is a hint of doubt on Bond's ambivalence on his sexual orientation as Bond retorts, "What makes you think this is my first time?" The new Bond maintains the tough exterior, but is a vulnerable human inside. This can be an inspiration for a modern day manager in today's world where empathy is regarded as more important than IQ in achieving success. The softer image has become equally important and there are many scenes in *Skyfall* showing Bond with a human touch and even some frailties, touching a chord with the modern audience.

In fact in our present, complex and global work environment empathy matters even more. Work has changed in so many ways to favour empathy as a core essential trait for managers. There are several examples of global leaders who have genuinely implemented this in their leadership styles.

Indra Nooyi, the CEO of Pepsi has set an agenda of 'performance with purpose', which is focused on delivering sustainable long-term growth while leaving a positive imprint on society and the environment. She has articulated it by stating, "Performance with Purpose represents our fundamental belief that in the 21st century a good company must also be a good citizen." This agenda has moved employees from merely having a job to living a calling. Indra is known to connect with employees in a free and forthright manner — singing with them in the hallway and interacting with people all along. In one instance, she wrote to the parents of 29 Pepsi executives telling them that they had raised great kids. Yet another example is that of Alan Mulally, the former CEO of Ford. He was known to walk around the company's corporate campus interacting with employees and had given several handwritten notes to them, praising their work.

With the rapid spread of social media, we now live in the 'like' economy, where every action needs an instant approval from peers and friends. Ironically, in this connected world, the need for high EQ in business leaders and its application in the work place has increased dramatically, as employees look for a sense of purpose in their jobs. A high level of EQ is a critical factor for the success of any leader!

Youth market

The famous vodka martini, which was a staple diet in all the Bond movies, has given way to Heineken beer. The old Savile Row suits of Bond have been replaced by the modern, contemporary fit of Tom Ford suits. Some of these changes are sacrilegious to old Bond loyalists, but are clearly more appealing to the younger audience. An important lesson for any company is that it needs to ensure that its products and services connect with the younger audience and change its offerings accordingly.

The new Q is cool, collected and tech-savvy, even challenging Bond with the cutting retort that he can do more damage sitting in his office on a computer than Bond can, in a year in the field. The pair of the new Q and Bond resonates with the challenges faced by many companies. This method of combining the youth with experience has been adopted by many start-ups across the world.

In many cases start-up founders are young, inexperienced and come with a vision to disrupt existing businesses. What they clearly lack is experience and this is made up by the guidance provided by a person who has been in the field for long; a person who can help navigate the intricacies of running a business. Hence, the model of 'mentors' or 'advisors' has now evolved into a well-established framework. These mentors have the requisite knowledge and experience and can guide and handhold young founders on a regular basis. It is a 'win-win' model and provides the correct roadmap for success.

In fact it is not uncommon to adopt this model even for established companies. Google famously brought the experienced Eric Schmidt on board to provide 'adult supervision' for the young founders, Larry Page and Sergey Brin. Schmidt had joined the company as CEO in 2001 and after stepping down from this position in 2011, continues as Chairman of the company.

Irrespective of the stage of growth of a company, a good blend of youth (innovation) and experience (knowledge) is the most potent combination for any company operating in a tough market environment.

Change management

The older Bond movies were based on the Cold War and the Russians and North Koreans were shown as arch-enemies, pitted against allied forces. This was but natural given the fact that James Bond was conjured by Ian Fleming in 1962 after his stint in the Second World War in the British Naval Intelligence. With the end of the Cold War, the *raison d'être* of James Bond was over. And yet, a lot of Bond movies did stretch the Cold War tensions as much as possible.

Until *Skyfall!* In *Skyfall* the Bond theme was clearly reinvented and Cold War tensions were replaced to focus on the more modern-day issue of terrorism.

In a telling statement, M, the head of MI6 deposing before a committee consisting of ministers, justifying her intelligence outfit mentions that, "…our enemies are no longer known to us. They do not exist on a map. They are indiviuals." She winds up her arguments by asking – "How safe do you feel?" And immediately after that, Raoul Silva (the villain in *Skyfall*, brilliantly played by Javier Bardem) walks into the courtroom with the sole intention of shooting down M. A shootout in a courtroom in central London where a villain coolly walks into the courtroom with a gun after killing the guards was inconceivable in the Bond movies of the past. In the older movies the battle was invariably fought in the field, in strange destinations – definitely not on home ground! But doesn't the courtroom scene resonate with modern day terrorism that does not owe allegiance to any country? In an earlier sequence the global headquarters of MI6 in London is attacked, reinforcing the fact that the enemy will not engage on the field but strike with impunity at the core – a far cry from the Cold War!

Drawing parallels to business, it is obvious that for any organisation living on its past glory, this is an important lesson of change management. Market environments change rapidly and adaption to the new reality is critical. What worked yesterday need not necessarily work today and certainly not tomorrow!

A good example of change management is an initiative done by Lafarge India, called Project Abhilasha. Lafarge is a global leader in building materials and in 2008 its Indian subsidiary acquired the concrete business of Larsen & Toubro and catapulted the company to become a market leader. Having gained market leadership, it realised that the demand for ready mix cement was growing and the market dynamics was altering rapidly with expansion by other players, rapid commoditisation and low price bidding.

Through its Abhilasha initiative Lafarge identified the need for delivering value added products, with a vision of positioning itself as a provider of high quality products. It wanted to emerge as the most reliable partner, offering innovative solutions through high performance teams. The company identified the need for greater customer focus and adaptability to a dynamic external environment. A new organisation structure was formed to improve customer connect and effectiveness. Also, the transit mixers and plant silos were upgraded to reflect the international brand image of Lafarge and a detailed segment-based marketing plan and branding architecture was created. The company also used the Large Scale Interactive Process (LSIP), whereby there was focus on planning and implementation of change in a short period of time. This project was successfully implemented with an enhanced brand image of Lafarge and an improved customer satisfaction of more than 90 per cent. Responding to the changing market scenario, Lafarge proved the point that change is essential in the lifecycle of any company and if it is handled well, it can make a remarkable difference to the company. With the successful implementation of this project Lafarge had proved that change management can be successful, if implemented properly.

Performance orientation

"Take the bloody shot!", barks M at Naomie Harris as Bond is fighting a terrorist on top of a train. M knows full well that it is not a clean shot. In an earlier scene, M orders Bond to leave a bleeding agent and chase a terrorist who is escaping with a hard disk drive containing names of all operatives. And when M is struggling with the crisis at MI6 and is offered a voluntary retirement with full dignity, she says firmly, "To hell with dignity; I will leave when the job's done."

If a job needs to be done, it has to be done in a cool and calculated manner. This is aptly displayed in *Skyfall* and is a useful example of the need to focus on results and outcomes for companies operating in a world of huge competitive pressure. Achieving the stated targets and reaching the top performance levels should be pursued single-mindedly in the work place.

From a sedate culture of fixed salaries with steady increments every year, corporates have rapidly moved on to a variable compensation model skewed towards performance. In sales-focused companies, the compensation model of the sales team is typically designed in a manner where around 40 per cent of the compensation is linked to the achievement of specific revenue targets. In fact, even the non-sales staff have variable pay, linked to specific individual and company targets often called KRAs (Key Result Areas) or KPIs (Key Performance Indicators). When one of the world's leading software companies started its operations in India, it designed a model where 80 per cent of the compensation of the sales staff was linked to numbers. There was a sweetener as well – if the sales person exceeded his revenue targets, there was a 25 per cent multiplier!

Compensation based on performance is a huge, irreversible trend amongst all progressive companies. It works well with the young workforce which prefers a strong co-relation of pay to performance. Indian companies are also warming up to this trend. In fact, Indian IT companies have been known to follow a rigorous performance appraisal process, following up with people who are below the watermark for minimum performance, asking them to leave. Financial services companies and start-ups are also known to be equally aggressive on under-performers. Many companies from other sectors are following suit. Performance orientation is here to stay.

After the success of *Skyfall*, the last Bond movie *Spectre*, was released in November 2015. The 24th movie in the Bond franchise and the most expensive one ever made, Sam Mendes continued as the director for *Spectre*. Having reinvented James Bond in *Skyfall*, Mendes chose the path of continuing the new avatar of Bond with further evolution of the process of reinvention in his second Bond movie. So, while Bond girls remained, Monica Bellucci in *Spectre*, is the oldest actress to be cast as a Bond girl (she is 50!); signalling that Bond girls need not always be in their 20s.

James Bond risks his palate by ordering a vegetable juice, when he visits the clinic in Austria to meet Dr Madeleine Swann (played by Léa Seydoux). And finally, in a cool move, he drinks vodka straight from the bottle, appealing to the young audience, but almost unthinkable for the Bond purists.

An interesting example of showing continuity of the process of the reinvented Bond is the climactic scene in *Spectre* where Bond has the option of shooting the villain, Ernst Blofeld (played by Christoph Waltz, looking woefully un-menacing), but he opts not to pull the trigger. This harks back to what M had told his new boss earlier, that "not pulling the trigger" is as important as "pulling the trigger". Bond then, quietly moves on, leaving the villain to his fate, holding Léa Seydoux in an almost Bollywood style finish of a happy ending, thus again displaying his high EQ.

Within this broad framework, *Spectre* has raised and continued to tweak some issues relevant to the times we live in. What is the role of backroom boys? Has it changed in the 'brave, new world'? Also, after dealing with the issue of terrorism in *Skyfall*, what is the new contemporary issue in *Spectre?* And more importantly, can the corporate sector glean anything from this movie?

Front-end vs backroom?

In *Spectre* the backroom guys go into the field, forced to tackle an emergency. Q travels to Austria to help Bond. M takes a gun and goes into battle on the field in the climactic scene and Moneypenny also joins the action. All this was unthinkable in old Bond movies

– for e.g., Q never moved out of his office and was always surrounded by his innovative gadgets; Moneypenny monitored schedules sitting at her desk; and M stayed at the central control room directing from afar.

With the increasing use of technology the front-end interface often becomes an app or a site and the back-end then becomes the front end – handling enquiries, ensuring a robust supply chain, handling customer complaints etc. E-commerce companies have realised the need for massive investment and efforts in back-office resources. The distinction between Sales and Support functions will gradually reduce and even support staff will need to go into the field to get real customer experience.

There are many examples of CEOs stepping into the marketplace and doing some active sales activity. As an example, on more than one occasion Flipkart's ex-CEO, Sachin Bansal would get out of his comfortable air-conditioned office and go out to actually deliver goods with his delivery boys, getting real world experience of the challenges faced by them.

In 2014, Tesco's then CEO Dave Lewis asked thousands of his head-office staff, including senior executives, to work one day a fortnight in the stores around the Christmas season. This initiative was called Feet on the Floor. Just as the backroom guys in the Bond movies are now getting on to the field to help Bond, corporates have to now realise that backroom guys can no longer be confined to the back-office. And in fact, it is essential that the back-room guys have a sales or field experience, so that they get first-hand experience of ground realities and improve their quality of service.

Privacy

In *Spectre*, Andrew Scott playing the role of the new head of British intelligence – C, as he is referred to – propagates a centralised worldwide program of surveillance and information gathering, to be shared between various countries. The new M (essayed excellently by Ralph Fiennes) is shown as a grumpy person, battling the bureaucracy of a new intelligence arm. In an interesting scene, M is appalled at the fact that surveillance is also done on the agents of MI6 and calls it "George Orwell's worst nightmare".

Privacy is now a global issue and got international attention with the Edward Snowden saga. After exposing the top-secret mass surveillance programs of the US and British governments, Snowden reaffirmed what he and many others of his ilk fundamentally believe – privacy is sacred and the tenet of a free society. They believe that governments should not monitor each and every mail and communication of private citizens. Taking up a contemporary theme, *Spectre* has taken a 'pro-Snowden' slant, showing the potential for abuse of State scrutiny and the increased need for cyber-security.

This new breed of 'hacktivists' – hackers who are activists – born in a digital era in chat rooms have provoked many probing questions. Is privacy sacred? Should access to all data only be with the government?

Should you be protected from surveillance by the government? With the ever-increasing security threats across the world, surveillance of data is also justified by governments on the assumption of the need for intelligence gathering, data mining and prevention of security threats. But, who will take the call?

This debate rages and has been brought out well in many scenes in *Spectre*, with C favouring complete control and access to all information, and M battling for a mid path. The jury is still out on what is the right approach and it might be a while before there is consensus on this across the globe.

With the rapid proliferation of data, data security and privacy is one of the most significant issues facing companies across the world. In June 2016, CISCO released a report titled *The Zettabyte Era – Trends and Analysis*, which has some amazing facts on data trends. Sample this – in the next four years data traffic will double. Annual global IP traffic will reach 2.3 ZB by 2020, when a million minutes of video content will cross the network every second, and it will take five million years to watch the amount of video that will traverse the global IP networks each month. With this massive explosion of data, companies need to ensure that there is a proper strategy to implement data security, privacy and integrity. It is also imperative to comply with regulatory issues and have a robust model of corporate governance.

Just a few years back, data was critical to only a few back-office processes such as payroll and accounting. Today it is central to any business and the importance of managing it strategically is only growing. It is so critical to decision-making that new-age companies often refer to it as the new 'GOD'!

With so much of personal data floating on the net, the debate is now focused on who 'owns' personal data. The business models of many global companies like Facebook or Google are based on analysis and exploitation of data. Indeed, personal data is the new currency of the digital economy. As custodians of personal data, these companies continue to create value for themselves from exploitation of the data and they have a responsibility to keep it secure and manage it responsibly.

When Apple launched its iPhone 6S in 2015 with enhanced security features, it sparked the debate of privacy versus public safety. In this phone, Apple employed a default encryption system that prevented both Apple and government authorities from accessing data stored on the device. Apple's commitment to privacy was tested when law enforcement agencies asked the company in February 2016 to unlock a phone, which was used by one of the shooters in a horrific shooting incident in San Bernardino, USA. Tim Cook, the CEO of Apple, refused to co-operate saying that it was a defense of civil liberties. In an email addressed to his employees Cook said, "At stake is the data security of hundreds of millions of law-abiding people and setting a dangerous precedent that threatens everyone's civil liberties." Apple has a stated policy of protecting the data of their customers and it is important that all companies have a well-defined policy for this which reflects their vision and mission.

Intuition

In the ongoing war of words between C and M in *Spectre*, C declares that double-0 agents like Bond are antiquated. In a globally networked world C questions the relevance and importance given to field agents. This is countered by M who asks if C had killed anyone in the field. He emphasises the importance of field experience and the need for intuition and human intervention in a critical situation.

Judgment and intuition are important traits of leaders and in fact the full potential of data analytics can be unravelled only when both are used judiciously. Based on intuition a hypothesis can be developed and tested with the use of data. There are many examples of how companies with large amounts of data still use intuition to take critical decisions.

Sebastian Thrun, a Google Fellow and Stanford professor, led the self-driving car project at Google based on his intuition that self-driving cars were possible, well before the necessary maps and data were available. He lost his best friend aged 18 in a car accident, and this inspired him to invent a car which could drive itself and was safer than the ones driven by a human driver.

In 2003 when Reliance Communications wanted to enter the telecom market in India, the late Dhirubhai Ambani is believed to have told his sons that they should make a phone call cheaper than a post card, and only then will it usher in a revolutionary transformation in the lives of millions of Indians. Based on this intuition, Reliance introduced call rates of 40 paise per minute at a time when the market pulse rate was ₹4 per minute. The company also bundled an affordable handset with a SIM card, costing less than ₹1,000 and created a revolution where ordinary people could afford a mobile phone. Today in India, many beggars also own mobile phones!

Away from business, in the cricketing world, M. S. Dhoni has proved that intuition is important in decision-making at critical moments in a match. Dhoni was one of the most successful cricket captains of all time, having tasted success in all formats of the game. Unlike other captains, he did not believe in complicating the game with excessive strategizing with data and statistics. In the T20 finals in 2007 with Pakistan, in a jaw-dropping move, he brought in the young and inexperienced Joginder Sharma to bowl that last over. Thirteen runs were needed in the last over and Joginder bowled out the last Pakistani batsman with three balls to go. Pakistan lost by five runs. Dhoni's intuition had paid off!

The legendary Ratan Tata has been quoted as saying, "There is an element of intuition in all of us, and you should let that play a role rather than just going with numbers. Most of the time, intuition shared with passion gives you the fuel to face the future."

Business leaders are sure to fail if they ignore intuition as part of their decision-making process. Neither an all-intuition nor an all-analytics approach will ensure success. A right mix of intuition and data-driven analysis is the best recipe for success. How to create the right decoction is up to the business leader!

To conclude

From the brilliantly shot opening scene set in Mexico till the climax in London, Sam Mendes has developed the reinvented Bond in greater depth in *Spectre*. Each Bond movie is a one-off adventure and in both the movies there is a constant questioning of the past and the need for 007 in the modern world. The new Bond has an answer to all that. Naomie Harris has aptly described the reinvention of Bond in *Skyfall* as "Old dog, new tricks". Reinventing a company or a product or a service is never easy. However, it is imperative in the increasing swirl of severe competition and rapidly changing consumer tastes in a globalised, socially-networked world. Reinvention does not mean discarding the old. It can be done with a good amalgam of the old and the new.

Both the movies were a big hit at the box office, with *Spectre*'s worldwide collections exceeding $800 million and *Skyfall's* exceeding $1 billion, proving the point that the reinvention of James Bond has worked. If James Bond can be reinvented, so can you!

KABADDI AND THE ART OF RESURRECTION

Kabaddi has been played in India for thousands of years. It is a high intensity contact sport which has originated from wrestling and requires no equipment – just a patch of ground and two teams of seven players willing to play the sport. The game is played in two halves of 20 minutes with a break of five minutes. Each team takes turns to send a 'raider' to the other half. The raider chants 'kabaddi, kabaddi' and attempts to tag one or more player in the other half and returns to his own half. The raider can be declared 'out' if the opposing team manages to wrestle him to the ground, before he touches the centre line. Despite being such an old sport, Kabaddi had a 'down-market' image and was watched by limited followers, with hardly any meaningful media coverage. In a cricket-obsessed country, kabaddi players were also poorly paid.

Given this background, the launch of the Pro Kabaddi League (PKL) in July of 2014 was a bold move to resurrect this traditional sport. Modelled on the lines of the successful cricket league – the Indian Premier League (IPL) – the format of Kabaddi was made slick and amenable to sponsorships and media coverage. Players entered the stadium to swirling lights, sparklers, loud thumping music and a cheering crowd – resonating the format used by WWE wrestlers entering a stadium. Instead of chanting 'kabaddi, kabaddi', an overhead screen had a count of 30 seconds. In the first three seasons, there were seven teams, some of them owned by Bollywood celebrities. It followed the caravan style format where all the teams travelled to a city and played for a period of over four days. By 2018 Pro Kabaddi is planning to increase the number of teams to 18 just like an international soccer tournament and also aims to increase its global reach.

In its very first season, Pro Kabaddi became a huge success. Stadiums were full, television viewership was unprecedented and sponsorships were forthcoming. Clearly, Kabaddi was resurrected and Indians lapped the new PKL format and enjoyed the 'Indianness' of the sport. Are there any business lessons to be learnt?

Fatigue

Any brand can face fatigue with consumers constantly demanding relevance and contemporaneity in any product or service which they consume. If this is not met, a brand can decline. There are many examples of how a fatigued brand has been resurrected – literally, come back from the dead!

The Lego group was founded in 1932 and was a leading toy manufacturer for decades. In 2004 it was nearing bankruptcy with huge debts on the back of declining sales triggered by the new trend of electronic games. The company cut its workforce by more than 1,000 and discontinued 7,000 pieces of unpopular toys. Lego has now been revived with a surge in sales and is back in the top rung of toymakers in the world.

Old Spice was a popular brand in the 1970s and has been around since 1938.

Associated with aging customers, it lost market share in the 1990s. Procter & Gamble acquired the brand and re-launched it as Old Spice Red Zone with a slew of advertisements targeted at the younger generation. These online ads went viral and the brand was revived in the US.

In India, the primarily carbolic Lifebuoy soap was repositioned as a family bath soap and is now a leading soap in this category.

Volkswagen's Beetle car first went into mass production in Germany in the year 1938 and became an iconic brand in the 1970s. After its enormous success in the 1970s the popularity of the Beetle receded. The old owners held on to their cars but new sales were getting increasingly difficult. The new Beetle was re-launched in 1998 and although its design was similar to the old one, the new model was much larger and had modern features like the touchscreen infotainment system. The new Beetle struck an emotional chord in many Beetle lovers and became a phenomenal success all over again. It is now the longest running and most manufactured car of a single platform; in fact, over 22 million Beetle cars have been sold. There are numerous active Beetle clubs across the globe. In the 1970s, ownership of a Beetle was associated with freethinking and was a statement of individuality and self-expression. This association still holds true today. Owners of the new Beetle associate the car with their old memories and Volkswagen has realised its potential in resurrecting the brand.

An interesting recent example in India is about Renault's foray into the Indian automobile sector. This merits a more detailed explanation for the journey traversed by the company. Renault entered India through a joint venture with Mahindra & Mahindra and launched a mid-sized sedan called Logan in 2007. This car failed miserably in India as consumers found the design too boxy and the price too high. This joint venture was called off and Renault re-entered the Indian market on its own in 2011 with Fluence and Koleos. These cars did not set their cash registers on fire either and Renault was looking to launch a car, which could become a volume-driver.

The Renault Duster was launched in India in July 2012 and has been a phenomenal success, having sold more than 180,000 cars since its launch. The Duster has won numerous awards including the prestigious 'Indian Car of the Year' in 2013. It was designed keeping in mind the needs of the Indian customer who wanted a car with the rugged looks of an SUV and the comfort of a sedan. Having tasted phenomenal commercial success in sales, Renault wanted to build a 'cool quotient' for the car. Gang of Dusters – G.O.D – was conceived — a short, catchy name with an easy to recall acronym. The Gang of Dusters initiative was launched in August 2013 and has caught the attention of all owners of the car. By becoming a member, an owner was entitled to various benefits. More than this, owners were entitled to join expeditions across various cities.

There have been numerous such expeditions and these have been hugely popular amongst the members. In each expedition, around 30-50 families join in with their Dusters. They drive in a convoy with planned halts along the way, adding to the adventure and conviviality. Clearly, the company has positioned the Duster as an expedition and adventure vehicle. They have effectively targeted the young consumers by creating a brand aura around G.O.D and have used the power of social media as well. On social media, they have a popular Facebook page and a Twitter handle (#gangofdusters) which has a large following. To complete this strategy, they have also launched an app for the Duster, which feature G.O.D. and other functionalities of the car.

Following the success of the Duster, Renault launched a small car – the KWID – in August 2016. This car was conceived in 2012 by Renault and 400 suppliers were identified locally to drive indigenisation. It became the first car in India to be launched with 98 per cent localisation and received 100,000 bookings in six months, aided also by some aggressive pricing. In financial year 2016-17, Renault sold around 135,000 cars in India, which is 88 per cent more than the number of cars sold in the previous year. With these cars, Renault has successfully resurrected its business in India.

Any brand with an inherent strength can be resurrected by ensuring that it is made more relevant to the younger generation – just like Pro Kabaddi.

Indianness

"You can take an Indian out of India, but you cannot take India out of an Indian" – this is a famous quote which was the theme of a well-known Franklin Templeton advertisement in India in the early 1990s. The same holds true for Indians living in India. The Indian consumer laps up any brand, which strikes a chord of 'Indianness'.

All the global fast food chains – McDonald's, KFC, Domino's Pizza, Dunkin' Donuts – had to alter their menus to suit the Indian palate. The Indian consumer will want the brand experience of a global brand with an Indianness to the food being offered. Hence, chicken tikkas and paneers have become an integral part of the menu of most international food chains in India, and beef and pork has been kept out. Interestingly, some of them have outlets that serve only vegetarian food, which is unique in their global network.

Starbucks sells a tandoori paneer sandwich and chicken tikka roll; Burger King has a Paneer King burger and KFC sells a Paneer Zinger. When McDonald's entered the Indian market, it realised that it could not sell its signature Big Mac beef burger and came up with its own product for India – Chicken Maharaja Mac. For their vegetarian customers, they offered Aloo Tikki burger, which had a cutlet made of mashed potatoes and peas with zingy Indian spices. They have recently added two Indian dishes to their breakfast menu – masala dosa burger and egg bhurji.

The clear success story in this space is of Domino's. It started operations in India in 1996 and could not make a big impact in the initial phase till it was reimagined and resurrected from 2006 onwards. Operated by Jubilant Foodworks in India, it crossed the 1000 restaurant milestone in February 2016, making it the biggest food chain in India and the only country outside of the USA to have more than 1000 restaurants. With an unprecedented market share of more than 70 per cent of the pizza market in India, it has presence in more than 230 cities across India.

Domino's re-worked everything for the Indian market and more specifically to cater to the burgeoning middle class. The toppings were altered to suit the Indian palate, with options of spicy vegetables and chicken. Indians love to share a dish that is ordered and eat with their hands – a cultural habit which was an amazing fit in the experience of eating a pizza. Another unique feature was a 'dine-in' place at their stores; this is unique to Domino's only in India. Eating a pizza was a dining experience and Domino's catered to this need of the Indian market by creating a space in their stores. In fact in smaller cities, this demand was so big that the 'dine-in' space was much larger. It also offered delivery within 30 minutes, which made it more predictable for the Indian consumer. It has recently launched a burger pizza – two pieces of pizza crust with a centre of cheese and pizza, instead of a patty – an interesting product that may chip at the burger market.

Domino's has also localised at just the right levels. They have figured that if they over-localise, Indian customers will not pay the premium associated with a western product and experience – for e.g. their dine-in stores have a spiffy décor with a lot of western influence. Domino's is an interesting case of resurrection of a brand on a platform of the appropriate amount of 'Indianness'!

To conclude

The success of Pro Kabaddi is attributed to the manner in which the sport was re-packaged, re-vamped and resurrected to make it aspirational and popular. The introduction of mats, its dramatic presentation and new techniques has metamorphosed the sport from a game of pure brawn to that of skill. In the inaugural season, the telecast of this sport was seen by more than 300 million viewers, second only to the hugely popular IPL. Over the four seasons, its cumulative viewership has witnessed a growth of 51 per cent, the highest ever for any sports league in India. In the recently concluded fifth season, 12 teams slugged it out over three months and according to the latest BARC ratings (Broadcast Audience Research Council) in India, the latest season garnered more eyeballs than the ongoing India-Sri Lanka series. No mean achievement that!

In another adroit move, the KBD Juniors program was launched which invited schools to participate – thus seeding its popularity at an early age.

With millions of viewers watching the sport on television and thousands of fans jamming the stadium, the success of Pro Kabaddi has proved that Indian consumers are willing to lap up products that are contemporary and have an Indian flavour. So, if you have a 'fatigued' brand, it is time to resurrect the brand, *a la* Pro Kabaddi.

F1 AND THE ART OF SPEED

F1 is a complex sport where up to 1,500 highly qualified personnel collectively design, develop and construct F1 grand prix cars, which race on 20 Sundays every year. The drivers have a superstar status and are instructed by engineers who try to extract the very best from their cars. It is the fastest motor racing series on the planet and these cars with the 1.6 litre hybrid engine put F1 well ahead of IndyCar and other motorcar races. The only other major global sport that can compete with this level of viewership is the Olympics and World Cup soccer, both of which last for just over a month.

Technology is used extensively in F1 racing where massive supercomputers perform billions of complex calculations to decide the positioning of parts, for something as seemingly insignificant as a wing plate. Gigabytes of data travel to a team's base, which could be located anywhere in the world, in order to take critical decisions. Some of the most cutting-edge car technologies are used in an F1 car, which may eventually land up being used in commercial vehicles. There are more than 20 examples of innovations used in F1 racing, which have been embraced in the real world outside of racing.

When you see an F1 race for the first time you wonder what is so fascinating about 12 cars zipping around a track for 90 minutes, with a maximum speed of 350 kmph, at a deafening sound of around 125 dB (a Boeing Jet makes a sound level of 150 dB at take-off)? How is it that the grandstands of every race are filled with passionate and crazy fans bedecked in team flags and merchandise hero-worshipping their favourite team and drivers? And how is it that there are more than 400 million television viewers in 187 countries, regularly watching F1 races over a period of 10 months?

And more importantly, is F1 only about fast cars, exciting drivers and glamorous girls? No. It is much more! It is about strategy, quick decision-making, teamwork and agility. Behind the glitz and glam there are serious team strategies that make all the difference. So, what lessons does it hold for all of us?

Competition

There is intense rivalry and competition between the drivers of F1 cars, even if they belong to the same team. During any race, F1 demands the very best from a driver in terms of skill and talent and the competitive spirit of the driver can make all the difference between a winner and a loser.

In the 2016 season, Mercedes cars were far ahead of the rest but the rivalry between the Mercedes drivers – Lewis Hamilton and Nico Rosberg remained unabated till the last race. As teenage friends, they were teammates in karting races in 2000; but when they competed in F1 races later, it was quite fierce.

At the start of the last race of the season of 2016 at Abu Dhabi, Rosberg had a

12 point lead and needed to finish in the top three to grab his first world title. Hamilton, a three-time world champion, was leading in the race, with Rosberg in the second place. In the final laps, Hamilton started slowing down on the turns to back Rosberg in the path of his nearest pursuers, Sebastian Vettel and Max Verstappen, hoping that they could overtake Rosberg and hand over the title to him. Hamilton even ignored team orders to speed up. Eventually, Rosberg came in second and won the world title.

The rivalry of Hamilton and Rosberg can now be counted among the great rivalries of F1, alongside Nigel Mansell and Nelson Piquet, Niki Lauda and James Hunt and Alain Prost and Ayrton Senna.

Similarly, in any market driven economy, relentless competition is inherent and unavoidable. Global CEOs often engage in skirmishes on Twitter and the new battleground for grabbing the consumer mind space is the social media. The stakes are high and there is never a let-up in the intensity. Some of the most famous global rivalries have been fought across different product categories – Coke vs Pepsi, McDonald's vs Burger King, Dunkin' Donuts vs Starbucks, Nike vs Reebok, Ford vs General Motors, Airbus vs Boeing and UPS vs FedEx. In each of these products, every decision is critical and a wrong move can give a huge advantage to competition.

Coke's disastrous efforts in the 1980s to tweak its popular formula and introduce a sweeter variant – New Coke – is an interesting example of how competitive fervour can sometimes lead to bad decision-making and loss of market share. Realising that Coke was losing market share to its rival Pepsi and feeling the intense pressure, Coke launched New Coke. Consumers revolted and more than 400,000 of them wrote letters of complaint to the company. New Coke flopped and sales of Pepsi zoomed. Recognising its mistake, Coke apologised to its customers, shipped Coke classic, withdrew New Coke and gradually regained some of the lost market share. Had Coke persisted with the New Coke, one wonders how much market share Pepsi would have garnered.

The Coke vs Pepsi rivalry continues unabated even today. From celebrity endorsements to chasing primetime television slots across the world, each company is trying to outdo the other. However, the new trend in the US market is to have healthier drinks, like energy drinks, juices and iced teas. Pepsi has made big investments in this space. Will Coke follow suit? Follow this space!

In any race, an F1 driver needs to be careful with every move to keep competition at bay. Similarly, CEOs of companies like Coke need to inculcate a high level of a competitive spirit and ensure that each of their strategic moves gives them a bump-up over competition and not the other way around.

Safety, safety, safety

F1 was always considered a dangerous sport and drivers and viewers knew the risk to life.

In the 1970s there was at least one fatality every year. The tragic death of three-time world champion Ayrton Senna in a crash at Imola in 1994 led to several changes focused on giving prime importance to driver safety. Safety is now at the centre-point of racing and all decisions are taken to ensure that the driver's safety is paramount.

Medical facilities are now compulsorily available at all tracks and there are reams of pages on safety regulations. From a fire-resistant suit to bespoke fireproof underwear and helmets made from fire-resistant Kevlar, all precautions are taken to ensure a driver's safety. In fact, every car has to pass a total of 18 safety tests before it can be taken out for pre-season testing. These tests are steadily increasing in rigour over the years.

One of the most innovative safety devices is the Head and Neck Support (HANS) device that connects to the driver's helmet. The HANS system prevents a stretching of the vertebrae and helps stabilise the driver's head during an accident. Introduced to F1 racing in 2003, it is now widely used across many forms of motorsport. All these safety features exacerbate the driver's discomfort, making it excruciatingly hot in the cockpit. During the race which lasts around two and a half hours a driver can potentially lose up to six pounds through sweating.

An interesting example of the obsession to safety standards is the recent incident on 7 April 2017 at the Chinese Grand Prix at Shanghai. The second practice session was called off after it was found that should there be a medical emergency, the medical helicopter could not have landed at the hospital in downtown Shanghai due to immense smog.

This overwhelming obsession to safety holds interesting lessons for the corporate sector. In F1, winning a race is the end purpose but not at the cost of compromising on safety. Similarly, for corporates, maximising revenue and profits may be the end purpose – but should it be achieved by compromising the real mission of a company? What is the real mission of a company? Is it trusteeship? Is it sustainability? Is it being a 'responsible company'? Once any company defines this, it should form the core of the company's operations and the entire organisation can be steered towards that path.

An interesting case study is that of HCL Technologies which adopted the mantra of "Employees First, Customers Second" (EFCS). Between 2005 and 2010, HCL's CEO Vineet Nayar, embarked on a mammoth effort to transform HCL into a high-performing organisation. He made a simple premise: put employees first! He believed that HCL could create a culture that attracted and retained creative employees. Putting the customer second may sound unconventional, but it worked. The financial results were impressive: a 35 per cent growth in revenue per employee and a sector-leading 25 per cent compound annual growth rate (CAGR) through 2008 to 2010. He then authored a critically acclaimed management book *Employees First, Customers Second: Turning Conventional Management Upside Down*, which has sold more than 100,000 copies.

Sir Richard Branson, founder of the Virgin group has echoed the same sentiments and is quoted in an interview with Inc., as saying: "My philosophy has always been, if you can put staff first, your customer second and shareholders third, effectively, in the end, the shareholders do well, the customers do better, and you are happy."

The Tata group has outlined its purpose as follows, "At the Tata group we are committed to improving the quality of life of the communities we serve." Just as safety is the central theme at F1 racing, the Tata group will have "improving the quality of life of the communities" they serve as a central theme. Everything else becomes subservient to that!

Speed

In the year 2010, refuelling in a pit stop was banned due to safety concerns. Now, a pit stop is done merely to change tyres and every car has to make at least one pit stop in a race. When the car comes into the pit, all four tyres are changed, damaged parts are replaced and front wings are adjusted – and all this happens in a matter of seconds. Each pit crew comprises more than 20 people and each mechanic is trained for a specific role and they take their obsession with fitness and diet as seriously as the drivers of F1 cars.

Constant and incessant drills at the factory and during practice rounds ensure that by the time they are at the race weekends, they have done hundreds of pit stop practices to the point that it becomes almost instinctive. The stakes are high and a delay of even one-tenth of a second can cost a podium finish. Due to constant innovation, the time taken to change all tyres has come down dramatically.

On 19 June 2016 during the F1 European Grand Prix held in the city of Baku, Azerbaijan, at the end of lap 7, Felipe Massa driving in his Williams car, came for a pit stop and the team released him after a stop of – hold your breath – only 1.89 seconds, as per the onboard sensors on the team. All teams are now working to break the 2 seconds barrier on a continuous basis. Some of the teams have also claimed that they have done pit stops of 1.83 seconds in practice stops that are not timed. For anyone watching a live race, it is a case of 'blink and you will miss it'!

All engineers have to work in unison and speed and agility is the key. There is a constant quest for innovation to shave off even one-hundredth of the lap time. Now, shouldn't the corporate sector learn a few things from this? In an era where much of the communication and decision-making happens though emails, the speed of response is critical. If it takes less than two seconds for a crew to change four tyres, can we justify a delay beyond 24 hours in responding to an email?

In an interesting case of the transfer of knowledge from F1 to real-life situations, team Williams has been assisting the neonatal team at the University Hospital of Wales (UHW) in Cardiff, United Kingdom, to help apply their F1 pit stop knowledge to the procedures used in the resuscitation of newborn babies. Both the scenarios require a team of people to work seamlessly in a time-critical and limited space environment. After visiting the Williams' factory and observing the pit stop practice, the hospital has started implementing a number of changes to improve its resuscitation process based on F1 racing. The resuscitation equipment trolley has now been streamlined to ensure that everything can be located as quickly as possible. Also, like the customised floor map that the Williams team takes to the races to map out the specific pit box requirements at each track, the hospital also has a standardised floor space mapped out in the delivery theatres to clearly show the area where the neonatal resuscitation team can work.

In fact, the Williams team has developed a device, known as Babypod 20, which helps to keep newborn babies safe during emergency transportation. Made from carbon fibre — the same material used in F1 cars' bodywork, it can withstand a 20 g-force impact and provides newborn babies with a secure, temperature controlled environment for ambulance transportation. These pods are now being used by UK's Children's Acute Transport Service.

51

In another interesting example, McLaren have applied data management and race simulation expertise to help London's Heathrow airport reduce the time spent by planes circling overhead and improve movements on the ground.

This process of the pit stop in F1 could have an application in many real-life business-critical situations. Retail stores could probably improvise on the process of handling peak consumer traffic, especially during festive seasons. Companies like Amazon, Flipkart and Alibaba face a huge surge in demand during specific seasons and could learn a lesson or two in the swift management of logistics in their warehouses. In China there is a recent trend of single people celebrating 11 November every year as 'Single's Day'– an antithesis to the Valentine's Day. Due to this, on 11 November 2017, Alibaba got an eye-popping revenue of $25.3 billion, making it the largest 24-hour online sale in the world on that special day. Do e-commerce companies use pit-stop techniques used by F1 teams in their fulfilment process? Probably not! Should they? The answer is obvious!

Timing

Since refuelling of cars has been stopped, the timing of the pit stop is one of the most important features of the race and it involves a lot of detailed calculation. When a car comes in for a pit stop, the other cars in the race will gain over the halted car. However, the car that makes the pit stop will run faster on the race-track than cars that did not make the stop, with lesser wear and tear on its tyres, providing more traction and allowing higher speeds along the corners.

Normally, race teams plan a pit strategy prior to the start of every race. There is a schedule for each car's planned pit stop during the race, which will take into account factors such as rate of fuel consumption, weight of fuel, rate of tyre wear, the effect of tyre wear on cornering speed and even expected changes in weather and lighting conditions. The pit strategy is calculated carefully so that the amount of time to be 'given away' to other competitors in pit stops is balanced out by the time gained while on the track, resulting theoretically in the shortest possible time to cover the scheduled distance.

However, a team's pit strategy is not a fixed, immutable thing; it is subject to change during the race, to take into account the unpredictable events that can happen, including the strategies followed by other teams. If there is any accident or the track is waterlogged after heavy rain, the race director can bring in the safety car to reduce the speed of the cars. When the safety car is on the track, cars cannot overtake and have to maintain their position till the exit of the safety car from the track. During this period, many cars head for the pit stop hoping to take advantage of the slowed pace to reduce the ground lost to other teams while making pit stops. The teams will then recalibrate their pit strategy to optimise it for the remaining race distance after the stop. Each car needs to use at least one of the soft tyres ('option' tyres) and one harder ('prime' tyres) during the race. If it rains, wet tyres can be used. With so many variables, the timing of a pit stop and its strategy plays an extremely critical role and can even decide who wins the race.

Similarly, in business decision-making, timing is everything! A sound decision that is delayed serves little purpose and similarly, a bad decision taken in a hurry can be disastrous.

The recent mid-term poll in the United Kingdom is an interesting example of poor timing. On 18 April 2017, Prime Minister Theresa May called for snap polls on 8 June 2017 as she wanted to silence her critics by hoping to get a majority for her ruling Conservative Party. The election results were a disaster for her party, as it lost many seats and led to a hung parliament. In fact, one of the leading dailies in UK gave an interesting headline 'Gamble in April costs May in June'. May's timing of her decision to go for mid-term polls had backfired!

Nowhere is the 'timing' decision more important than in the film industry, where the decision on the date of release of a movie becomes extremely critical. Since the huge success of *Jaws* in the summer of 1975 and *Star Wars* two summers later, big Hollywood movies line up their releases in the United States during summers. Similarly, Bollywood movies also follow a well-planned strategy for finalising the date of release of their films.

Salman Khan, the Indian superstar, always releases his films every year during the Eid weekend. Any other film released during this time will need to compete for an audience with Salman Khan's movie. There are many festival holidays in India and seasons like the Diwali holidays see a crowding of movie releases. The summer holidays in India are also considered a good time for release of movies. However, they now have to compete with the cricket matches of IPL, which have become popular and draw a significant audience.

An interesting trivia is associated with the day of the release of a movie. Why are most movies released on Friday? One reason could be because Friday is the last working day of the week and the weekend collections become critical, especially when the movie is released across hundreds of screens with multiple shows in multiplexes. Eventually, the producer of a movie has to decide on the timing of the release of the movie, after considering various factors – the holiday season, the release of other movies, other significant national events and competition for audience-attention from other sports like cricket. Ultimately, timing is everything!

Real-time decision-making and analytics

There are many variables and possible scenarios during an F1 race – weather, accidents, car safety and tyre degradation. During each race, a team has more than

50 analysts crunching information on a real-time basis to provide analysis to the race engineers and the team director. More than 120 sensors on each car send back 15 to 20 MB of real-time data during every lap. Whilst the data is analysed and crunched by experts, it is the Team Boss who has to make a decision in split seconds.

Interestingly, in 2014 KPMG and McLaren forged a 10-year strategic alliance to use McLaren's predictive analytics and technology to KPMG's audit and advisory services. McLaren's sophisticated predictive analytics could be applied to many business issues and other than its alliance with KPMG, its expertise has been used in improving R&D and manufacturing processes, creating air traffic scheduling systems and optimising production processes.

As corporates start paying more attention to analytics, many of the techniques and processes used in F1 racing could find a place in the decision-making process.

To conclude

The aim of any F1 team is to win the race. Behind the drama of a podium finish, there is a lot of sweat and toil of thousands of mechanics, team engineers and analysts, who work tirelessly to save that tenth of a second, which will give their car an edge over the others. Each team has budgets running into hundreds of million dollars to innovate on the latest technology for each part of the car. Many of these technologies overflow into commercial vehicles and the processes followed by the teams can be applied in business conditions.

More importantly, any F1 race holds important lessons to business leaders on a host of issues – teamwork, timing, innovation, competition...and above all, the speed of decision-making. Ultimately, a podium finish in an F1 race will not happen just because a team has a superior car and a superb driver. Strategy is the key to winning!

HARDIK
AND THE ART
OF METEORIC
RISE...AND FALL!

Born on 20 July 1993, Hardik Patel hails from an average middle class family from Viramgam near Ahmedabad, in the state of Gujarat. After his schooling in Viramgam, he joined the Bachelor of Commerce (B.Com.) course at Ahmedabad's Sahajanand College and after an average academic record, graduated with 50 per cent marks. During his college days, he was elected to the post of general secretary of the college students' union and was active in the activities of the union. At the young age of 19, Hardik joined the Sardar Patel Group (SPG), a non-profit social organisation headquartered in Gandhinagar and within a month, became president of its Viramgam unit. However, within three years he was ousted from his post due to an internal conflict with a senior leader. Hardik felt that the affirmative policies were not benefitting his community and formed the Patidar Anamat Andolan Samiti (PAAS) and became its convenor, claiming that Indian independence movement leaders like Mahatma Gandhi and Sardar Patel had inspired him.

Hardik Patel suddenly shot into the limelight when he mobilised half a million members of the Patel community at a rally in Ahmedabad on 25 August 2015 to agitate against reservations. Before this, no one knew who Hardik was. So, how did a 22-year-old get so many followers and such massive media attention? What is the secret of his sudden rise from obscurity? Are there any lessons to be learned in the meteoric rise of Hardik Patel?

Hardik comes from the Patidar community that constitutes 12-14 per cent of Gujarat's population. The word 'Patidar' literally means landowner. Anandiben Patel the former Chief Minister of Gujarat is a Patidar. Many members of this community are affluent and have been successful in business. Despite all this, Hardik has raised the issue of inclusion of the Patel community in the category of Other Backward Classes (OBC) and, concomitantly, inclusion of this community for reservations in educational institutions and government jobs. But then, how can a community which is relatively well off, demand reservations?

Hardik has argued that the Patel community is disadvantaged from the moment they seek to join a good college. Despite securing high scores they do not get admission as they do not have seats reserved for them. He is quoted as having said, "A Patidar student with 90 per cent marks does not get admission in an MBBS course, while SC/ST or OBC students get it with 45 per cent marks." He insists that his movement is not against the SC/ST or OBC communities getting their due, but about Patidars getting their share as well. Hardik argues that this disadvantage continues beyond the educational platform as well, as people from his community later seek jobs in the government. According to Hardik, the private sector has not been able to provide enough jobs for the Patels who rightly deserve it. Although a sizeable portion of the community is in business and is well off, there is still a large number that struggles with these inequities. Responding to all these problems,

Hardik has an earthy logic – there are many who suffer along with the Patels and, hence, all reservations should be removed. As a society, we should value work not caste, he argues. "Free all, or enslave all of India", he says.

The subject of reservations is a deeply emotive issue and when Hardik started his agitation, he managed to strike a chord with his community and motivated them to protest. Identifying a deeper connect with the people and understanding their problems is the key to success and Hardik showed how he could mobilise half a million protesters by doing exactly that. He spoke their language, which may sound coarse, but he articulated a logic which they understood and motivated them to protest – which they did in an unprecedented manner.

An interesting example of a company, which has a good connect with its customers, is that of Maruti Suzuki. Founded in 1981 as Maruti Udyog Ltd., its aim was to provide an affordable car to the masses of India. At inception, Suzuki had a minority stake of 26 per cent in this public sector undertaking. Over a period of time, the government diluted its stake and by May 2007 it had sold its entire stake to public financial institutions and Suzuki had a majority stake in the company. Starting with its small Maruti 800, the company had a glorious ride in India and by February 2012, it had sold its ten millionth car. Despite the entry of many car manufacturers in India, Maruti Suzuki now has an unprecedented market share of around 51 per cent.

One of the main reasons for its success has been its high customer connect. It has more than 3,000 service stations across the length and breadth of the country, providing coverage unmatched by its competition. The company now has a car for every section of the society from middle class to upper middle class. Interestingly, it has started chipping at the higher end market with cars sold through its premium brand outlet, Nexa. Even in its lower versions, it offers good value for money, with bells and whistles like screen infotainment system, which is provided by others in higher end versions. Its model of service excellence ensures high customer satisfaction levels and repeat buyers. Driving a strategy of 'high volume, low cost' and consistently pushing for high customer satisfaction, it has managed to deliver cars which have been lapped up by the Indian customers – proving that a strong connect to customers and their needs always pays higher returns!

Flaunt it

Hardik is young, brash, willing to speak his mind and was just 22 when he addressed the massive rally in Ahmedabad in 2015. At another rally in Gujarat he made a fiery speech and was seen, controversially, with a gun in his pocket. When asked by the media about this image of a gun-carrying Patel, Hardik was unfazed and said that carrying a weapon was a symbolic gesture, meant to protect his community from oppression. In fact, in response to a specific question by a television channel, Hardik mentioned nonchalantly that he would carry an AK-47 if the government allows its possession.

In August 2015 he travelled to Delhi to seek a larger support from the Jats and Gujjars for his movement and after his speech he brandished a sword. In a sense he epitomizes the young Indians who are willing to carry their attitude on their sleeve and appear decisive and strong. Hardik belongs to a new-age generation where aggression and flaunting of aggression is the norm.

In the same vein, there are many start-up entrepreneurs who are similar to Hardik, willing to speak their mind and face competition head on. You often hear the promoters of Flipkart and Amazon India having a go at each other in public — threatening to dislodge the other. Sample this: in October 2016, after the conclusion of the biggest week-long online sales, Flipkart and Amazon India had similar sales figures, with Flipkart taking a minor lead, claiming to have sold 15.5 million units against Amazon's 15 million. However, Flipkart was not happy with these numbers and their erstwhile CEO Binny Bansal took a potshot at Amazon, saying that selling churan (mixture of powdered ayurvedic herbs), hing (asafoetida) and prime memberships do not constitute real sales. Amazon India's CEO Amit Agarwal countered by saying that people bought mobile phones, TVs, home appliances or fashion and also bought churan and hing! He also added that e-commerce in India was at an inflection point and the online purchase of daily-use items was becoming a habit.

Rahul Yadav, the displaced founder of Housing.com, never shied away from speaking his mind. Twelve IITians, including Yadav, started Housing.com in June 2013.

One of the many controversial acts of Yadav during his stint as a CEO, was to tender his resignation to board members and investors accusing them of not being "intellectually capable of any discussion". It was withdrawn within five days and Yadav apologised for his statement. Yadav also famously gave away his entire stake in the company, then valued at ₹1,500-2,000 million to the 2,000 plus employees as a gift, saying he is only 26 and "it's too early in life to get serious about money." Soon thereafter, he challenged Ola's founder, Bhavish Aggarwal and Zomato's founder, Deepinder Goyal to also give away half of their shares to employees. Yadav's histrionics are not unique and are symptomatic of the younger generation wanting to flaunt their attitude.

In the cricketing world, India's star player, Virat Kohli, is known for his aggression on the field. Considered as one of his greatest strengths, Virat is not overwhelmed by any opposition and plays with aggression. Most traditional Indian cricket players are calm and do not speak to the opponent unless provoked – not Virat! He loves to play an aggressive type of cricket and often engages in verbal duels when provoked. Virat and his ilk believe that you should be aggressive where required and flaunt your abilities.

Interestingly, at an Economic Times event in June 2015, Kunal Shah the founder of Freecharge had the audience in splits when he mentioned that his team calls anyone above the age of 35 'uncle' and he was one of them. With the average age of start-ups being in the 20s, the prevalent work culture is vibrant and full of fun; companies run by older people are referred to as 'uncle companies'. This behaviour of the young workforce clearly shows their attitude and confidence, which results in aggressively flaunting their capabilities – much like Hardik Patel!

Failed strategy

Hardik's rise was meteoric and the question on everybody's mind was – will he fade away like a meteor? Or will he use the platform to launch a sustainable movement and become a glowing star? To come to where he had reached, Hardik had used coarse language and rustic logic. But to go to the next level, he would require more sophisticated political skills and a certain finesse. Like many companies need to, Hardik ought to have changed his strategy to make it to the next level. Unfortunately, he did not.

Slighted by the huge rally in Ahmedabad in August 2015, the Gujarat government constituted a committee headed by a senior cabinet minister to look into the demands of PAAS and the Patidar community. Hardik and his supporters met the Chief Minister on 14 September 2015 and during the meeting, Hardik put forth a litany of demands, other than reservations. He emerged from the meeting, threatening to do a 'reverse Dandi Yatra' from 19 September. The Dandi March had always been associated with Mahatma Gandhi's act of non-violent civil disobedience, when he set off from Sabarmati ashram to reach Dandi on the coast of Gujarat to protest against the levy of tax on the manufacture of salt by the British rulers in India. The 24-day march by Gandhiji had started on 12 March 1930 and accompanied by his followers, Gandhiji had walked 390 kms to reach Dandi on 6 April 1930. At Dandi, in open defiance of the rule imposed by the British authorities, salt was made and Gandhiji emerged victorious.

Using the symbolism of the Dandi March, Hardik announced a reverse Dandi Yatra which would start from the coastal village of Dandi and end in Ahmedabad. By doing so, Hardik had broken the first unwritten rule of negotiation – not to start something new when discussions are in progress to resolve an older issue! This was his first misstep and the start of his fall.

The government decided that it was time to come down with a heavy hand and used its machinery to prevent the reverse Yatra from taking off. Section 144 of the Criminal Procedure Code was clamped, preventing the assembly of more than four persons at all locations where Hardik and his supporters were likely to meet. Hardik panicked and kept changing the launch pad of his Yatra. Eventually, around 50 people gathered at Surat's Patel-majority Varachha area and the police whisked away 30 of them and kept them in police custody for the day. From a rally of half a million in Ahmedabad in August 2015, to merely getting the support of 50 people in September 2015 – Hardik had seen a meteoric fall! After that the Gujarat police tracked all his rallies and promptly arrested his supporters when they found that any activity was being undertaken without the requisite permission, thus asphyxiating Hardik's movement. The final nail in the coffin was Hardik's arrest on 19 October 2015 on charges of sedition, for his alleged advice to his supporters to kill policemen rather than commit suicide to demand reservation. He was also charged with insulting the national flag during his lacklustre agitation to stop the India-South Africa cricket match in Rajkot.

Hardik finally got bail in July 2016 with a condition that he would stay outside of Gujarat for 6 months. He stayed in Rajasthan for 6 months and returned to renew his movement. However, by this time the number of his supporters was far lesser and the high pitch of his movement had subsided. Hardik still has an opportunity to rise again. He needs to follow a completely different strategy now – which will need to be more nuanced, astute and mature, rather than protests and disruptions. Will he change his strategy and rise again? Only time will tell!

The rise and fall of Hardik has many lessons for corporates. What works in the initial launch and rapid growth phase is unlikely to work in the next phase of consolidation. Take the example of Sony Corporation of Japan. In 1979, it unveiled the legendary Walkman and created a massive revolution in the way in which everyone interacted with music. Across the world, consumers wanted to lay their hands on this device, which allowed them to carry their music in the form of analog cassette tapes wherever they went. It was the 'Apple' of that time. Following the Walkman craze, Sony again changed the entire face of audio recording when it teamed up with Philips to introduce the compact disc media format to music lovers.

The quality and quantity of music on a CD far outstripped that of the cassette tape and again Sony had taken a leadership position in the world of media consumption and was sitting pretty, with a bit of overconfidence and smugness. They did not realise that there were dramatic new products being developed by competitors, which would change the landscape and threaten their leadership. On 23 October 2001 Steve Jobs announced the launch of the iPod and this marked the precipitous fall of Sony. By giving consumers a device with the ability to listen to innumerable high quality audio songs on the go, Apple had upended Sony's leading position. Clearly, Sony had allowed its leadership position to slip by, remaining a complacent leader and not spotting new trends. Whilst Walkman saw the rise of Sony, iPod ensured its dramatic fall!

Snapdeal is another example of the meteoric rise and fall of an e-commerce unicorn. Originally started as a daily deals site in 2009 by Kunal Bahl a Wharton graduate and Rohit Bansal an Indian Institute of Technology Delhi alumni, it morphed into an e-commerce site and was valued at $6.25 billion at its peak. In August 2015, Kunal Bahl the CEO, claimed that his company would topple arch-rival Flipkart from its perch at the top of the Indian e-commerce market within six months.

At its peak, Snapdeal made a series of errors. It hired thousands of employees in an unplanned manner over a short period of time and as it expanded rapidly, it lagged behind Flipkart and Amazon on customer satisfaction. In September 2016, it spent more than ₹2,000 million to launch an expensive re-branding exercise to transform its image, as it looked to stay relevant in the bitter market-share battle with larger rivals – Flipkart and Amazon India. Sales did not pick up in the festival season of October-December 2016 and in fact, it started tanking in the months of January-March 2017. With this near death experience, Snapdeal had no choice but to cut hundreds of jobs and slash spending and throw in the towel. Their shareholders even tried to merge with Flipkart, but called off the negotiations in August 2017 after seven months of intense dialogue. From its rapid rise as one of India's most valuable e-commerce unicorns, Snapdeal has seen a precipitous fall and has now decided to pursue an independent path.

To conclude

Hardik Patel's meteoric rise and eventual fall has interesting lessons for the corporate world. It is essential to constantly evaluate strategies which have worked during the rapid growth phase and re-align them to ensure that it does not lead to a precipitous fall. In all likelihood, the strategies employed in the phase of rapid growth are unlikely to succeed in its next phase. Re-calibration of strategy is required, particularly when a company has witnessed rapid growth and has leadership position. Ironically, a company is probably most vulnerable when it is at its peak.

To ensure a long-term growth, a meteoric rise needs to be handled carefully to avoid a sharp fall, *à la* Hardik Patel.

ALEXANDER AND THE ART OF WAR

The son of King Philip II of Macedonia, Alexander was born around July of the year 356 B.C., into a family that traced its royal roots back to the great hero Hercules. King Philip gave Alexander the best possible training from his trusted and skilled veterans in swordplay, archery, horsemanship and all the other skills required in war. King Philip also realised the importance of honing the intellect and wanted the greatest minds of that age to train Alexander. He turned to Aristotle, who was trained under Plato, who in turn had trained under Socrates. Aristotle was a genius and invoked curiosity in the mind of Alexander. With his vast breadth of knowledge, Aristotle made a deep impact on the mind of Alexander who applied this knowledge in later years during his reign over his large empire.

At a young age Alexander became the king in a sudden and unexpected manner. He started his campaign for extending his empire at the age of 20 and continued his battles for 12 long years, conquering Greece, Persia, Central Asia and finally reaching India, where he fought the famous Battle of the Hydaspes with King Porus on the banks of the river Jhelum. For a Macedonian King, India was the last frontier and after reaching India, Alexander had to reluctantly return home with his war-fatigued army. It was during his return journey that he died suddenly from an unknown illness.

By the time he was barely 32, Alexander had conquered the entire known world at that time, with his empire extending from

Macedonia to India. Indeed, Alexander the Great was one of the most brilliant war generals of all time and the strategy lessons from the art of war as practiced by him in two of his historic battles are analyzed here.

Agility

The Battle of Gaugamela was one of the most interesting battles that Alexander fought where he displayed his valour, confidence and application of a superior strategy. Gaugamela was a huge plain of land, with an open space for a battle. On one side was King Alexander with less than 50,000 of his men and on the other was King Darius with more than twice the number. Alexander knew he had to do something different to win the battle. During the strategy sessions with his generals, he felt that the only way to win the battle would be to find a gap in the formation of the huge army of King Darius and swiftly move into it.

Alexander had made his soldiers nimble-footed by replacing the traditional heavy armour with a much lighter version and a small shield. The soldiers could now move swiftly in any direction and change course before the enemy could react, making them truly agile and Alexander realised that he could exploit this advantage in the battle.

After the troops were lined up facing each other, Alexander did something which completely perplexed King Darius and his generals. Instead of striding straight across the plain, he rode with his horse towards

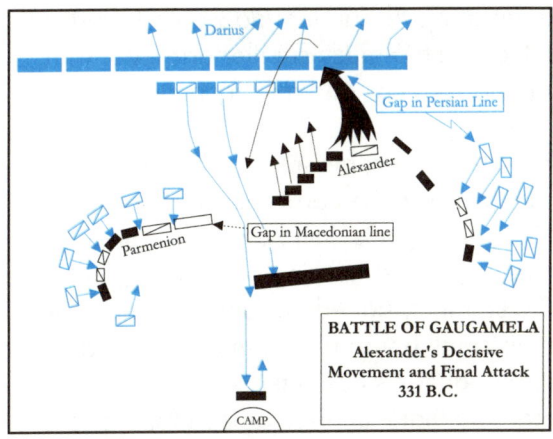

BATTLE OF GAUGAMELA
Alexander's Decisive
Movement and Final Attack
331 B.C.

the far right of the battlefield. Seeing
Alexander and his men riding towards the
right, Darius ordered his cavalry to move in
that direction to try and stop him. As he was
riding, Alexander saw the thinning of Persian
soldiers and suddenly turned to change
direction. With the agility of his men who
had light armour, Alexander moved into the
gap created in the Persian lines with speed
and alacrity and reached within sighting
distance of Darius. The Persian cavalry with
its heavy armour could not manoeuvre with
the same efficiency. Darius was caught totally
by surprise and ordered his charioteer to turn
and flee from the battlefield.

Alexander wanted to pursue Darius and
capture him alive. However, he had no
choice but to turn back and help his soldiers
facing the larger army. With their King having
fled, the Persian soldiers faced inevitable
defeat. Alexander fought a larger army by
finding a gap in their line-up and exploited
it to the fullest. Also, he used the advantage
of a smaller and more agile army, by making
movements that could not be matched by a

larger army. Alexander had won a historic battle – with a much smaller army, but with superior strategy and military brilliance.

An interesting comparison of the use of such tactics in the corporate world is by Nirma detergents. In 1969, Karsanbhai Patel, a chemist working with the Gujarat Government, started packing a formulation in his small house and named the powder Nirma, after his daughter Nirupama. Realising that there was a need for a good value product, he priced his detergent powder at ₹3.50 per kg as against ₹15 per kg of Surf by Hindustan Lever Limited (HLL).

The use of detergent powder was pioneered by HLL's Surf in 1959 and within a few years it had a dominant market position. When Nirma was introduced in the market, it went almost unnoticed by HLL as it was a low-priced item. And this is precisely the strategy that made Nirma hugely successful! It discovered its own space in the market dominated by HLL and introduced a product at a price-point that was affordable to ordinary, middle-class Indians.

The initial market of Nirma was a non-user of Surf but as its reputation spread, Surf users also started to try Nirma which was associated with the concept of 'value for money'. Against the huge resources of HLL, Karsanbhai had found an opening, which he exploited. He did not take HLL head-on and being a large organisation, HLL was not agile enough to react with alacrity. On the other hand, Karsanbhai was not burdened with the bureaucracy of a slow-moving large company and quickly became a huge success.

With its success in the detergents market, Nirma proved its agility by launching soaps and personal healthcare products. The Nirma group is now a multi-billion dollar revenue group and has shown how it is possible to succeed against a large company with a dominant market share, by finding a gap in its marketing strategy and moving in with agility with a product that the consumers want.

This story is now being repeated regularly in the marketplace with the new tool which large companies laggardly adopt – digital! In every consumer segment, there are digital companies that are upending the rules of the game for established companies. When Karsanbhai introduced his detergent powder, he did not have the benefit of a powerful digital technology. Today, Uber has the largest number of cars without owning a single car and Airbnb has the largest number of rooms without actually owning a single one. In fact, technology has made it easier for agile tech-driven start-ups – the digital Davids – to take on large, bureaucratic, slow moving Goliaths. Large companies will inevitably have some gaps in their coverage, which can be easily exploited by nimble technology-driven companies. The story gets repeated in each product and service category.

The element of surprise

Another interesting battle of Alexander is the one he fought against King Porus of the

Paurava kingdom. This battle took place on the banks of the river Hydaspes (now known as the Jhelum, a tributary of the Indus) in Western Punjab, at a location in modern day Pakistan.

Both the armies were lined up against each other on the banks of the river Hydaspes, which was deep and fast-flowing. Alexander kept Porus guessing for many months by moving his units back and forth across the shore across many miles. Alexander realised that the odds were against him as any direct attack had little chance of success and he had to use 'surprise' as a strategy to get close to the enemy troops.

Alexander used a suitable upstream crossing, many miles away from his main camp. When the word reached Porus that a large force of Macedonians was crossing several miles away from the main camp, he sent his son to stop them.

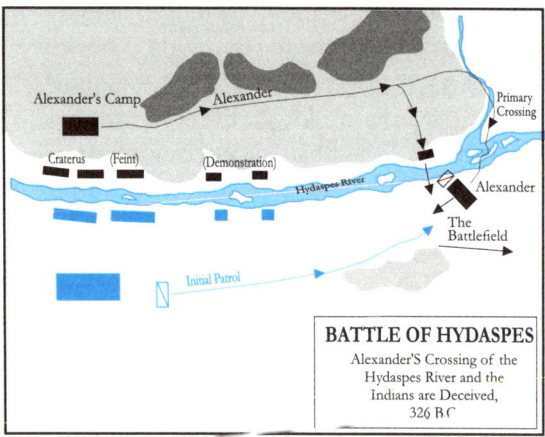

Alexander and his troops quickly routed the young son of Porus. On hearing the news that his son was dead and that Alexander had landed on his side of the river, Porus followed with the main force of his army. Seeing Porus moving his troops, the remaining troops of Alexander crossed the river towards him. Alexander then deployed a classic 'pincer' strategy to surround the enemy. While his main army attacked from the front, Alexander sent his cavalry to the left and the right, with orders to come up behind Porus and his troops. Porus was surrounded on all sides and fought bravely atop his war elephant, until he was defeated. Alexander sent an envoy to Porus and when they met, he marvelled at the six-foot tall man, who kept his head high even in defeat. Alexander asked him how he would like to be treated, to which Porus replied, "Like a King"!...words that have been etched in history!

Pepsi successfully used Alexander's strategy of 'surprise' as an important element in the business battlefield in its ongoing cola war in India. During the 1996 Wills World Cup cricket tournament in India, Coke paid a handsome amount to become the official tournament sponsors and advertised heavily using this as their tagline. However, it did not anticipate Pepsi's surprise move, when the latter launched a marketing campaign with the tagline "Nothing official about it", implying that no one really cared which drink was the official sponsor to the tournament, because Pepsi would be a natural choice for a soft drink. This advertising campaign created media history and was one of the most successful advertising campaigns of that decade. 'Surprise' as a strategy worked for Pepsi!

An interesting variant of the 'pincer strategy' was adopted in the battle over cafes in India. Barista started its first outlet in February 2000 at Basant Lok, New Delhi. With an increasing disposable income and a global trend in coffee consumption, Barista identified an opportunity where coffee lovers sought a complete experience. They positioned their cafes as places where people would meet for the love of coffee and their target audience was the age group of 14-60 years. Their logo and design had shades of orange and brown to promote a laid-back atmosphere. Barista expanded rapidly and opened 100 outlets in India within a few years (200 at present), and Sri Lanka and Dubai as well.

Café Coffee Day (CCD) opened its first outlet in 1996 at Brigade Road in Bengaluru. CCD had a youth orientation with its target market of 15-29 years and products priced at an affordable level. Their logo used bright red colours with a stroke of green and their stores had a vibrant decor, reflecting the young target audience. Barista had taken a lead over CCD and CCD realised that it had to do something different, and so used a variant of the 'pincer' strategy.

Barista had done the tough job of creating an awareness and market for coffee drinking. CCD now started locating their stores in the proximity of existing Barista stores. In fact, at Bandra bandstand in Mumbai, a CCD store is separated from the Barista store by a wall! CCD was successful because it gave an affordable option to people who had wanted to enjoy some coffee at a lower rate.

With many CCD stores in close proximity, Barista was left struggling to keep pace with this massive growth and had no space to manoeuvre. CCD had used a 'pincer' strategy by surrounding the existing stores of Barista with its own stores and offering the customers better value for money.

Today, CCD is the largest coffee chain in India with more than 1,400 stores and around 500 Value Express outlets. It also has a presence in a few countries outside India and had a successful IPO in October 2015. CCD's example is an interesting case study of how a brand can unsettle an existing brand and then leave it with little place to manoeuvre – a true application of the 'pincer' strategy in the marketplace.

To conclude

Alexander fought and won many battles in his long campaign of 12 years. In each of his battles, he won because of his application of superior strategy. Alexander led from the front and motivated his men to fight and win battles that looked unwinnable. At the core, there was intense planning, deep thought and superior strategy, which was different in each of his battles. The strategies he adopted can be applied in real-life business situations and are relevant even today – facing competition, product launches and entering a new market segment. As businesses face challenges on a daily basis, a lot can be learnt from Alexander and his art of war!

SOCCER AND THE ART OF WINNING

The FIFA World Cup is the biggest sporting spectacle in the world. The cumulative audience of all matches of the 2014 World Cup was estimated at around 26 billion and more than 700 million watched the finals. Thirty-two teams including the host nation compete in the tournament at venues within the host nation over a period of a month. The 2014 FIFA World Cup tournament was held in Brazil and Germany won the finals on 13 July 2014, beating Argentina in a dramatic goal in extra time. Any victory or defeat of a team evokes profound emotional responses from its fans and soccer fans are known to be the most fanatical.

Each team comes into the game with a well-thought strategy, carefully studying the strengths and weaknesses of its opponent. Can we glean some business strategies from these soccer matches?

Predictability

Spain entered the 2014 World Cup as favourites with an impeccable record of being the only team to have won three international tournaments in a row: the Euro 2008, the World Cup in 2010, and the Euro 2012. Spain boasted of several legends, including midfielders Xavi Hernández and Andrés Iniesta, who had perfected the tiki-taka style of playing soccer, which more or less means touch-touch.

The tiki-taka style of play involves holding possession of the ball for large portions of the game, moving the ball quickly from one player to the next in quick successive short passes. The key strategy is to keep the ball away from the opponent and then deliver the killer pass to score a goal.

What followed in the group stage sent shockwaves through world soccer. Spain was outscored 1-5 by the Netherlands in their opening match; they lost 0-2 to Chile; and salvaged some pride by a victory over Australia. The Spanish team was resting on its laurels, suffering from success fatigue and playing a football game strategy which was known and predictable to its opponents. The tiki-taka style had brought success to Spain over time, but in this World Cup it had outlived its purpose.

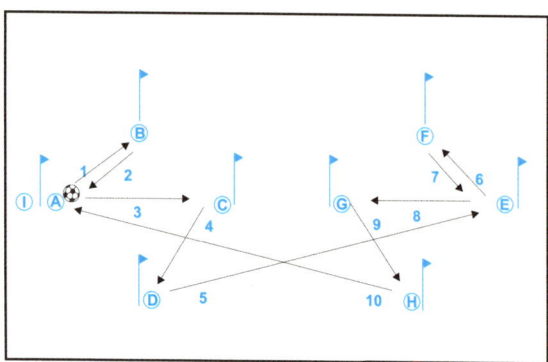

This has many lessons for successful companies who do not alter their strategy in a rapidly evolving and fiercely competitive market. Leaders in any segment can fall into this trap of infallibility, repeating strategies which have worked in the past and made them successful. Just look at how some e-commerce companies (Flipkart, Amazon) have created a buzz and posed a serious threat to many established brick and mortar companies. The tiki-taka style of older companies may not be relevant in the digital world and must be replaced.

Motivation

The English team had many well-known players made famous by the popular English Premier League. However, the team had a dismal performance and did not make it to the last eight. The team seemed to lack motivation to succeed.

On the contrary, the US team played like a well-knit team with a strong desire to win. In the critical match against Belgium, they narrowly lost 1-2 to Belgium. Tim Howard, the goalkeeper of the US team was the hero of the match, making a record 16 saves. Asked to comment after the match Tim Howard said, "I was merely doing my job. This is what I had signed up for." They lost the match, but won the hearts of everyone with their doughty spirit and a never-say-die attitude.

Motivated people define the difference between success and failure of a company. No sector has understood this better than the IT industry in India. It has grown into a phenomenal $118 billion industry in a short span of 25 years by focusing strongly on world class HR practices and keeping its workforce motivated. These companies provide a range of facilities at their campuses, creating an aspirational image for a job with them.

Risk-taking

In the finals, Joachim Löw the German coach made a late substitution by sending 22-year-old Mario Gotze, telling him -"Show the world you are better than Messi." Mario scored in the 113th minute of the match and created history.

In a crucial match against Costa Rica, the Dutch coach Louis van Gaal substituted the goalkeeper Jasper Cillessen and sent Tim Krul in the dying minutes of the match. As the shocked spectators watched the penalty shoot-out, Krul saved two penalties and ensured that Netherlands moved into the semi-finals.

Risk-taking is fundamental to business. However, imagine changing the sales strategy in the last month of the financial year to prop up sales! Software companies are known to make some enticing offers to give momentum to their year-end sales.

Car companies are also increasingly concocting new schemes on their slow-moving cars in the last days of the financial year. It requires courage to make a sudden change in strategy in the final moments of a financial year, which can sometimes make a difference between a winner and the second best.

To conclude

The popularity of soccer is increasing every year and FIFA looks to increase viewership in the two largest markets in the world – India and China. Once it gains popularity in these markets, there is no looking back.

Soccer is an extremely competitive sport and teams have realised that every game is important and winning is impossible without a proper strategy in place. Even the favourite team sometimes struggle against the lesser known teams when playing some crucial matches. Soccer is a sport not just of skills, fitness and talent – but application of intense strategy. Companies can draw some useful lessons in the art of winning from soccer!

BAAHUBALI
AND THE ART OF
THINKING BIG

"Why did Kattappa kill Baahubali?" – the final scene of the first part of the magnum opus *Baahubali* ended on one of the most tantalising junctures in recent cinema history, with a question left unanswered for two years. Interestingly, the makers of this movie not only managed to keep the answer under wraps, but also sustained the interest in the story.

Baahubali is the most ambitious film ever made in India's film history. It has surpassed all earlier movies in terms of scale, grandeur, special effects and cost. The two part epic fantasy has been co-written and directed by the acclaimed filmmaker, S. S. Rajamouli. It is a story about the royal family of the fictitious kingdom of Mahishmati. Spread over three generations, the story revolves around how the good royals are dethroned by another branch of the family. In the final scene of the first part, Katappa, the royal family's loyal bodyguard, kills Amarendra Baahubali, the virtuous royal and leaves the audience in a state of shock. The second part unravels the sequence in which Mahendra Baahubali, son of Amarendra Baahubali, seeks retribution.

The first part, *Baahubali: The Beginning* was made at a cost of ₹1,800 million, the most expensive Indian film at the time and created a record at the box office, with massive collections of ₹6,500 million. The second part, *Baahubali 2: The Conclusion* was even more ambitious and expensive and was produced at a cost ₹2,500 million – an absurdly high amount for an Indian film.

When the movie was released, it created box office records across the globe, being the only Indian film that has generated gross collections of more than ₹10,000 million.

So, what were the reasons for the success of *Baahubali?* And more importantly, are there any lessons that we can glean? Are there any *"Baahubalis"* in the corporate and other sectors?

Big is beautiful

The entire movie was shot with an unparalleled access to resources at Ramoji Film City in Hyderabad that spans over a hundred acres of land. In fact, some scenes required a farmland and 20 acres of land was cultivated with maize crops to get an authentic shot. For most of the shooting, there were more than 2,000 artistes on the set and thousands of VFX shots (visual effects) were used in the film. In fact *Baahubali 2: The Conclusion* was made in Telugu and dubbed in Tamil, Hindi and many other languages. It was released in April 2017 in 9,000 screens across the world – truly unprecedented for any Indian movie. Both the movies were made on a massive scale for the global audiences with the hope and expectation that they will also reap in huge commercial success. 'Think BIG' was their mantra!

An interesting example of an organisation from India that is on the global map is ISRO (Indian Space Research Organisation).

ISRO is under the administrative control of the Department of Space, Government of India, and has achieved many significant milestones since its establishment in 1969. It built India's first satellite Aryabhatta, which was launched by the Soviet Union in 1975. In 1980, it launched Rohini – the first satellite to be placed in orbit by an Indian-made launch vehicle, SLV-3. Since then, it had a string of successes with the launch of many rockets.

One of its most significant achievements was the launch of Mangalyaan on 5 November 2013. This Mars Orbiter Mission (MOM) probe was successfully inserted into the Mars orbit, making India one of the few countries in the world to have achieved the capability of entering the interplanetary space. Built at a cost of $67 million, it is around one-tenth the cost of similar missions of NASA, USA. ISRO is the fourth space agency in the world to have successfully undertaken a mission to Mars and the first agency to succeed in its maiden attempt to reach Mars. In fact, on February 2017, ISRO set a new record in space mission achievement when it successfully launched 104 satellites at one go.

ISRO has demonstrated that an Indian organisation can build world-class capabilities and be at the cutting edge of scientific knowledge and technology. Space technology is complex and has been the domain of large countries. ISRO has joined the big league by thinking on a global scale and launching satellites and MOM, which would have been otherwise inconceivable for a country like India.

There are similar examples of corporates who have built capacities of global scale. Reliance Industries has built the world's largest single-site grassroots refinery at Jamnagar, in the state of Gujarat. The Tata group is a shining example of an Indian conglomerate with world-class capabilities. It consists of over 100 operating companies spread across six continents, with more than 60 per cent of its revenue coming from businesses outside India. Many of their group companies have achieved global leadership.

Tata Global Beverages is the second largest tea company in the world; Tata Chemicals is the world's second largest manufacturer of soda ash and TCS is the second largest IT services company in the world by market capitalisation and profit. All this proves that it is possible to 'Think BIG' and build global scale in any sector in India.

Suspense

The makers of *Baahubali* managed to keep the interest of the audience alive by finishing the first part with a sensational ending and leaving the audience gasping for more. When the second part was released, it almost seemed that the audience was waiting for it. *Baahubali* is not the first movie with a sequel, but is probably the only one that had such a stupendous suspense-filled ending.

In the business of television serials there is a surfeit of serials in India on various subjects from family drama to comedy. In fact, the regional channel serials are extremely popular with the regional audience and draw a large viewership. Many of the serials are broadcast over weeks and months and vie for audience attention. Other than good content, acting and overall quality of an episode, one of the most important pieces for the success of a serial is to ensure a repeat audience draw for its future episodes.

To do that, it is important to end an episode at an interesting juncture, which will keep the audience interested and eager to watch the next one. It is an art, which is critical to the success of the entire serial. Many of the television serial producers use it to good effect; however, the makers of *Baahubali* have shown how they have applied this art with amazing results.

One global company that appears to have mastered the art of keeping consumer interest alive is Apple. Every Apple product seems to marry art, design and technology and offers a unique value to the consumer. It is probably the only company in its space where consumers line up for days before the release of the product just to be one of the first few ones to lay their hands on the new offering. This has happened repeatedly for releases of iPhones, where there are serpentine queues outside the retail stores, days before the launch. Apple keeps the consumer interest alive by giving hints of the next product to be launched and creating a buzz around the possible features of the product. The company also has some limited releases, like the red coloured iPhone 6S, which was launched in March 2017. Its marketing campaign is also well crafted to stir up interest and desire in the product.

Apple has been extremely successful in keeping consumer interest alive in future product releases and many companies could learn a few tricks from them.

Originality

S. S. Rajamouli has admitted in an interview that he started reading *Amar Chitra Katha* comics when he was seven years old and was fascinated with the folklore, mythology, forts, battles and kings. These stories had a deep influence on him and *Baahubali* was inspired by all these stories of royalty and grandeur. *Amar Chitra Katha* is one of India's largest selling comic book series, with more than 90 million copies sold in 20 Indian languages. It was founded in 1967 and has more than 400 titles on Indian mythology, history, folklore and fables in a comic book format.

Baahubali's story of the royal family of the fictional kingdom of Mahishmati had all the trappings of an epic story – royals battling for the kingdom, extended battle scenes, political machinations in the royal court and the righteous royals battling to get back their kingdom – the audience lapped up every aspect of the story created by the writers of the movie. It was an original story which had been brought together elegantly on the big screen. Originality is important and nowhere is this more relevant than in the film industry. The success of *Baahubali* clearly proves that!

There are many success stories of products that have their original idea generated in India. The success story of Amul is probably the best testimony to this. The late Dr Verghese Kurien was the architect of Amul. He arrived in Anand, in the State of Gujarat, in 1949 as a government employee to manage a dairy and scripted Operation Flood, a cooperative movement that turned India into one of the world's two largest producers of milk.

Dr Kurien's original intention was to empower the farmers who had no option but to sell their milk at very low rates. He evolved a unique model of paying famers based on a transparent mechanism and creating a cooperative structure where the milk was bought and processed. Thus Amul (short form for Anand Milk Union Ltd) was born and its famous mascot of a girl in a polka dotted dress is popular even today.

The Gujarat Cooperative Milk Marketing Federation (GCMMF) was later established as an umbrella body to market milk and milk products, manufactured by the six district cooperative unions of Gujarat. GCMMF owns the Amul brand and it has successfully diversified from milk and butter to a whole range of products including chocolate, ice creams, paneer, health beverages and flavoured milk. It is India's largest food product marketing organisation with an annual turnover (2016-17) of $4.1 billion. It has an unprecedented 3.6 million milk producer members and its daily milk procurement is approximately 18 million litres. Amul is sold in India through a huge network of 100 million retailers and even after the entry of some foreign players, it has maintained its leadership position. GCMMF is India's largest exporter of dairy products and Amul is now sold in more than 50 countries around the world.

Started with an original idea by Dr Kurien to give economic freedom to farmers in Gujarat, Amul has morphed into India's leading milk brands and is also now making inroads in markets outside India. This model of forming a milk marketing federation owned by farmers was incubated in Gujarat and is now being replicated by farmers of many other states – truly proving that a strong, original idea can spawn huge success!

To conclude

The phenomenal success of *Baahubali* has proved that it is possible for Indian companies and organisations to 'Think BIG' and plan to capture global markets. Given a choice between envisioning a product or service for the national market, a company can opt to plan for a global scale. It requires a far bigger vision and planning and a bit of courage to put together the required resources. It will obviously need to be supported by a proper vision, detailed planning and immaculate execution. *Baahubali* was produced in the city of Hyderabad and has captivated audiences across the world. The success of the movie proves that there is a potential *Baahubali* within each company and organisation – all it needs is some global vision to make it successful!

KEJRIWAL AND THE ART OF SIMPLICITY... AND COMPLEXITY!

In a short span of time, Arvind Kejriwal has made a big impact on Indian politics. He launched his campaign of 'India against Corruption' in late 2010 and the fledgling movement received a huge boost when Anna Hazare joined it and began his hunger strike in April 2011 at Jantar Mantar, demanding the passing of a Lok Pal Bill. This hunger strike got a massive popular following and the nation was riveted with round-the-clock coverage of this event by the media. The mammoth numbers at his rallies clearly indicated that Indians were getting increasingly impatient with the ubiquity of corruption and yearned for change. With the support of Anna Hazare, Kejriwal had succeeded in bringing the issue of corruption to the forefront. His movement required a catalyst to kindle the issue and Anna Hazare had provided the required momentum.

The sudden rise of Kejriwal – a green horn in politics to the centre stage in Delhi – holds some important lessons for corporates. What were the reasons for his sudden rise? Did he follow a fundamentally good strategy? And was he consistent?

Riding the wave

Kejirwal was able to identify the deep angst of the Indian youth. People were fed up of the pervading corruption and the absence of a clean and corrupt-free politician. Kejriwal made this his central theme and it resonated very well with people, especially the youth. Kejriwal sensed that he had a right message for the masses and rode the initial wave of popular support.

This has interesting parallels to business – are CEOs able to successfully ride a business wave with the right offerings? A good example of this is the vision of the founder CEOs of the Indian IT industry. The Indian IT industry has become a massive $125 billion industry in a short span of about a decade, as it rode the outsourcing wave. The catalyst for this was the short-term opportunity of Y2K and outsourcing, which later mutated into large IT companies offering a wide range of IT services. Even as these companies are facing renewed challenges due to digitisation and global politics taking a far more nuanced stand on globalisation, they are looking to pivot their business models. Due to their rapid growth in the past decade, these companies now have massive resources at their disposal and are in a better position to ride the second wave hitting them now.

The recent push towards digitisation in India also has an interesting dimension. India is probably the only country in the world where the state and regulatory bodies are vigorously encouraging the adoption of the digital medium. In fact the big push was given by the sudden move to demonetise high currency notes, announced on 8 November 2016. Sensing an immediate opportunity, e-wallet companies put out huge advertisements and provided a massive marketing push. Other digital payment companies also realised that this was a huge catalyst to their business. With the shortage of currency notes, many people embraced digital payments and volumes surged to unprecedented levels. Demonetisation was exactly the catalyzing event – an almost surreal event – for digital payment companies. Post re-monetisation, the initial surge may have mellowed; but it did change the spending habits of many Indians.

Keep it simple!

During the Anna Hazare fast, Kejriwal had a simple message – anti corruption. The movement also proposed a solution in the form of a powerful Lok Pal. Post the formation of the Aam Aadmi Party (AAP), Kejriwal had promised a clean, open and transparent government. It was a simple and powerful message, which touched the inner chord of every Indian who was exasperated at having to deal with corruption. The modern Indian voter in Delhi had voted for a clean government and was not swayed with the politics of caste and community. In keeping with his simple image, Kejriwal always wore a simple outfit, shunning the traditional politician's attire or designer khadi.

Kejriwal had followed an almost naively simple strategy, which is called the KISS (Keep it simple, silly) principle in management jargon. Many companies have complex vision and mission statements, which are read and understood only by those who draft them. If the message to customers, shareholders and employees was simple to understand, its execution and success would be easier. Recently, the Mahindra group changed its tagline to "Rise". Simple, but powerful!

In the context of transparency, corporates could do a lot more to meet the increasing aspirations of stakeholders for good corporate governance. In the long term, good corporate governance will distinguish a good company from a company that is shunned by stakeholders. Kejriwal also adroitly used the social media to have a low cost, high impact communication to all his stakeholders – an important lesson for CEOs, who are still 'social media illiterate'. Based on this simple messaging and strategy, Kejriwal's AAP made a big impact in the elections to the Delhi assembly in 2015, winning 67 out of 70 seats – one of India's biggest assembly wins – which stunned the ruling party at the Centre.

However, over the past two years, he seems to have lost his way and the Indian voters have brutally punished him in the State assembly elections in April 2017. His party barely won 20 seats in the elections to the Punjab assembly and lost all the 39 seats where it had fielded candidates for elections to the State assembly in Goa. In fact, 38 out of the 39 candidates of AAP lost their deposits in the Goa elections – a candidate loses his deposit of ₹10,000 if votes secured are less than one-sixth of the valid votes. In his home turf of Delhi, AAP had to face a crushing defeat in the Municipal Council of Delhi elections, winning only 48 out of the total of 270 seats. After riding such a populist wave in 2015 with a historic win in the Delhi State Assembly, what went wrong? Did his simple message get convoluted?

Rapid fall

Arvind Kejriwal exploded on to the political scene as a challenger to the existing brand of politics. The Aam Aadmi Party that he formed, was associated with a transparent and corruption-free governance model.

People voted for him in the Delhi elections in 2015 as they felt that Kejriwal and AAP provided a credible alternative to the existing political scenario. Although the core issue of rooting out corruption still resonates with most Indians, Kejriwal rapidly lost his sheen and his narrative became muddled and complex.

Kejriwal started playing the 'victim'card, by portraying how he and AAP were willing to work and make a change, but the Union government was not co-operating and in fact, putting numerous road blocks to their implementation plans. They spent more than ₹900 million on advertisements to put forth this view! Kejriwal also dedicated a large amount of his 'air time' in personally attacking the Prime Minister and his policies. His public image as a 'people's person' was also dented when he was not seen in the capital city when it was reeling under the outbreak of dengue and chikungunya in 2014. All these strategies were different from his earlier simple strategy of a crusader of 'anti-corruption' with the ability to focus on issues that mattered to the ordinary Indian. The voters got a muddled message and handed AAP crushing defeats in the recent State Assembly elections.

The story of the rise and fall of French Connection, a UK based retailer of clothes and accessories, has interesting parallels. In 1991, the company started using the brand name fcuk – which was deliberately written in lowercase and looked similar to the taboo word. The fcuk campaign gained notoriety and spawned a range of slogans based on the fcuk strapline – e.g. "No time to fcuk", "Born to fcuk". Due to its irreverence, it gained a lot of attention and consumers lapped these T-shirts and more than one million of them were sold in a short period of time. The company was listed on the London Stock Exchange and valued at £500 million at its peak. It had a simple slogan – eye-catching and notorious! From those heydays, it has seen a steady decline and infact the last nine years has seen the company in red and market capitalisation dip to a meager £32 million. So, what went wrong?

There was massive counterfeiting and overexposure of the brand leading to its saturation – a victim of its own success. Also from their simple messaging and the successful campaign in the 1990s, French Connection could not evolve to the next level. It tried to expand its portfolio from men's shirts to accessories like watches, perfumes, belts etc. None of them set the cash registers on fire. Meanwhile brands like Zara rapidly moved in and caught the attention of the customers, further nudging out fcuk.

Another example of a rapid rise and precipitous fall of a brand is that of HMT watches. During its hey days, the company produced 116 million watches and was one of the world's largest manufacturers of watches. HMT (Hindustan Machine Tools) was set up in 1961 in collaboration with the Citizen Watch Company of Japan to become India's first wristwatch manufacturing company. Owned by the government, HMT watches were an instant success due to their simple design and durability for daily wear. There was a huge demand for these watches in the 1960s to 1980s, with an unprecedented wait list to buy them. In fact, the company had an advertising campaign with a slogan – "Timekeepers to the Nation" – a simple message, which resonated with the people, who lapped up the affordable and simple watches. HMT dominated the market with its mechanical watches. In the 1970s, it manufactured quartz watches and was unsuccessful due to consumer resistance for the higher price of the quartz watch from the HMT stable. The company then decided to stop selling quartz watches and refocused on the original mechanical watches. The Tata group established its watch brand under the name of Titan and started selling watches based on quartz technology. These trendy and fashionable watches caught the fancy of the consumers in the 1990s and Titan started nudging HMT from its dominant position. HMT belatedly tried to foray into the quartz segment but the consumer did not associate HMT with fashionable watches and its messaging got lost. HMT's decline was rapid and it finally closed shop in 2015.

To conclude

Arvind Kejirwal stormed into the Indian political scenario with the formation of AAP in 2012 and was enormously successful with his simple theme of driving out corruption. In the last couple of years, this simple message has become convoluted and the people are wondering what AAP really stands. Kejriwal committed many snafus – to name one – he shared the stage with Lalu Prasad Yadav, a consummate politician with his own brand of self-styled buffoonery and not known to be squeaky clean. He paid a price.

Kejriwal can still turn around the fortunes of his party by focusing on the simple message of 'corruption'. This is still an issue for ordinary Indians and if Kejriwal sticks to this, he could perhaps bounce back!

SAIRAT AND THE ART OF REGIONALISM

The total size of the Marathi film industry was estimated to be in the range of ₹1,500 million to ₹3,000 million. Was! Until the release of *Sairat*, the phenomenally successful movie, that has grossed more than ₹1,000 million! This movie was released in early 2016, with two young, raw and unknown actors in the lead and created a box-office record. It has been proclaimed as the most successful film in the history of the Marathi film industry. In rural parts of the state of Maharashtra the demand was so high that theatres had to slot shows at midnight and even 3.00 am in the morning – truly unprecedented!

What is even more interesting is that the movie was made on a shoestring budget of ₹40 million with newcomers Akash Thosar aged 22 years and Rinku Rajguru aged just 15 years. Filmmaker Nagraj Manjule wrote this simple story of a young boy and girl falling in love and set it against the backdrop of the contentious issue of caste discrimination. His earlier film *Fandry* which was his directorial debut, focused on a young boy's infatuation with a girl in a society ridden with caste-based discrimination. The budget of *Sairat* is a pittance of what is spent by Bollywood even on its low budget films.

Does this success of a regional film hold any lessons for us? In the rush for leadership in the big and glorious national markets, are corporate leaders missing out on some critical market segments?

Content is King

The success of *Sairat* clearly indicates that the Marathi film industry has a far greater commercial potential than originally estimated. *Sairat* has made a telling point to producers of Hollywood and Bollywood films – that a Marathi film made at a much lower cost can stand on its own and become a commercial success.

In the modern day Bollywood era of star-studded masala films with a massive commercial blitzkrieg, Marathi films have evolved their distinctive positioning. Directors of Marathi films have deftly dealt with several critical, topical and sensitive societal issues. In fact they have proved that the audience is prepared to appreciate such subjects. Most Marathi films have not been star-studded affairs and many of the actors are from the Marathi theatre. Manjule has gone a step further and chosen ordinary people to cast in his film. What emerges is that content is king in Marathi cinema. The audience is eager for a movie if it has a good story that is well presented. *Sairat* is an interesting example of how a good quality movie which is tuned to local content, can spin unimaginable profits in the regional space.

In the food sector, there are many examples of regional food outlets, which are popular because they cater to the local taste. Amba Bhadang, based in Kolhapur is popular for its Kolhapuri Bhadang, a spicy version of the traditional chiwda, an Indian savoury. With a legacy of 175 years, Babu Singh Pedha in Dharwad is famous for its sweat meat shop, made from the milk of local Dharwadi buffaloes. Arohan Foods from Guwahati is famous for its variety of tasty pork pickles. Started in 1947, Baba Thakur Das & Sons in Alwar is famous for its milk cake. In the small town of Sattur in the Virudhunagar district of Tamil Nadu, the century old M. S. Shanmuganadar Mittai Kadai is famous for its spicy snack, sevu.

There are many such cases of local food stores who are extremely popular in their region because they cater to the local taste with an extremely good quality. Content is, truly, the king!

Extending boundaries

Sairat was a big hit in the state of Maharashtra as it was filmed in Marathi, the language spoken in Maharashtra. To extend its reach beyond the traditional audience in Maharashtra the movie had sub-titles, making it watchable for audiences outside the state as well. It was released in more than 200 theatres outside Maharashtra in states like Karnataka, Kerala and West Bengal. In fact, it was also released in the UAE and in the US.

Sairat has proved that a good regional product can have a big market outside the region, if it is tweaked for an audience and a consumer group outside that region.

A good example of such a successful strategy – again in the food industry – is that of Haldiram's. This family business was started in 1918 in Bikaner when Ganga Bishen Agarwal began making and selling a new snack, the bhujia. His mother had given him the nickname Haldiram, and the bhujia he sold came to be known in the markets as Haldiram's bhujia. The name stuck forever! With its distinctive taste and flavour, this bhujia became extremely popular in Bikaner and the surrounding markets.

From these humble beginnings, Haldiram's is now a global brand with revenues of around ₹50,000 million and is managed by the grandsons of the founder. A perishable, local snack, was turned by the family into a national brand by increasing the shelf life, and focusing on packaging and branding! Along with bhujia, a range of Indian snacks are now available under the Haldiram's brand in vacuum-sealed packages and can also be bought online. These snacks are available in stores in India and many parts of the world.

Haldiram's has also opened a chain of fast food restaurants across India serving Indian snacks. From simple snacks, they have expanded the product lines to sweets, frozen foods and baked foods and now ventured into the Quick Service Restaurants (QSR) segment. This business is increasing rapidly and is already bigger than many international brands operating in India.

There are many regional players in India, with a strong presence in the regional space. With the advent of e-commerce, it is now possible for these players to continue their strong regional presence and expand their reach outside the region.

Localisation

In *Sairat*, the audience connected with the issues portrayed in the movie. Caste discrimination is still a big issue, especially in the rural areas, and the tumultuous problems faced by the young couple in *Sairat* from different castes were something the audience identified with. In addition, the movie was embellished with songs, which became a big hit. Localisation of a product to the regional market is critical.

Take the example of Cobra condoms, which are popular in some states in Northern India. This brand, along with Enjoy and Midnight belong to Anondita Healthcare, a Noida based company. Anondita sells more than 100 million pieces annually in the northern states of Delhi, Uttar Pradesh, Punjab, Haryana and Himachal Pradesh, making it the largest regional condom player. What makes regional players like Anondita tick? They supply a good quality product at a reasonable price, maintaining regular contact with the retailers who influence the decision-making process. Most importantly, these regional brands resonate with local imageries!

Reckitt Benckiser Group plc, the maker of the world's most popular condom brand Durex, which had a stagnant market share in India over the past many years, has recently launched an interesting product to compete with the large number of regional players. It will now sell condoms in sachets—small packaging that helped personal care product companies to get villagers to buy shampoo – at an attractive price of ₹25 per sachet, which is much lower than its normal price. Condoms have been traditionally sold in boxes printed with vibrant colours or pictures of scantily clad models. The advertisement campaign of the new Durex condoms features leading Bollywood actor Ranveer Singh and is targeted at the young generation. This is the first time since Durex was launched in 1997 that Reckitt Benckiser has lowered its prices, and is trying to shed the non-mass market tag.

Will this succeed against regional players like Anondita? Will Anondita compete with Durex in the premium segment? Will Anondita launch a similar product in a sachet? Durex has the marketing muscle to support its launch of the new product and Anondita is known to be agile in the marketplace with a strong accent on localising its product. How this battle pans out will depend on how Anondita responds to the new launch of Durex. It will certainly be an interesting space to watch.

Another example is Wagh Bakri tea launched in 1892 by Narandas Desai, a devout Gandhian. He started out with 500 acres of tea estates in South Africa and was later forced to come to India after facing racial discrimination. Wagh Bakri is now an extremely popular brand in Gujarat with a market share of more than 50 per cent in this state. With its distinct Gujarati name and an oxymoronic brand name, Wagh Bakri is now making inroads in other Western states. With revenues of more than ₹9,000 million, it is the third largest packaged tea company in India.

Vi-John is another example of a regional brand, which has now grown to a ₹5,000 million company. Founded in 1960, their shaving cream is the largest selling product in their portfolio of personal care products. Vi-John has made deep inroads in the north with its network of dealers and product offerings catering to the consumers.

Because of its diversity, the Indian marketplace is often compared to a continent rather than a classic nation state. It is a multi-ethnic, multicultural society in which more than 22 official language-groups co-exist, each with its unique customs but bound by a shared colonial history and contemporary political structures. Against this backdrop, marketers have to face the challenges of meeting the complex demands of both the urban and the rural consumers. In fact the challenge of marketing to the rural consumers is accentuated with the regional flavour of ethnicity, culture and taste. Hence, to be successful, localisation of a product is extremely critical – only then can you get a company's product to connect with the local people who will consume your product!

Value products

Sairat was a wholesome movie, with young lead actors and hummable songs, shot brilliantly in rural Maharashtra by Manjule and his team. Going to watch this movie in a theatre became a family party and a social event. Hordes of friends and families went together to watch the movie and many of them were seen dancing in the aisles when it was time for the famous *Zingat* song in the movie. As an entertaining outing this was a good 'value for money' proposition.

Regional consumers have evolved from an era of consuming low-quality, low-priced products to desiring 'value products' – a combination of utility, features, local design and aesthetics – all at a 'value' price. Another interesting trend is that the consumers in regional areas are increasingly mimicking the consumption patterns of the urban consumers. In fact, due to the increased reach of telecom, media and smartphones and its rising influence on consumption patterns, regional consumers now aspire for branded, high quality products and to make an informed decision, they seek information about a product through various sources – television, internet, SMS, chats and mobile phones.

The hard fact is that outside the urban areas there are 850 million consumers in India, residing in about 650,000 villages. These consumers form about 70 per cent of the population and contribute to around 50 per cent of the GDP(Gross Domestic Product). With such a massive consumer base, no marketer can ignore this huge market – as an example, the rural FMCG (Fast Moving Consumer Goods) market is expected to expand at a CAGR of 17 per cent to reach a market size of $100 billion by 2025.

A good success story is that of Vadodara-based Manpasand Beverages. In the highly competitive beverages market, it has revenues of more than ₹8,000 million and has constantly focused on regional markets, generating more than 75 per cent of its revenue from these markets. Founded by Dhirendra Singh, Manpasand Beverages started selling their beverage Mango Sip at a price point below ₹10 in villages in Eastern Uttar Pradesh, which already had established beverage brands like Frooti. Mango Sip became a huge success and is now their flagship product. Two years back they launched a carbonated fruit beverage,

Fruits Up, which now contributes to more than 20 per cent of their revenue. Manpasand's marketing and advertising spends are significantly lower than competition and it has a wide distribution reach in rural areas. It is now planning a juice at a price point of ₹2 to ₹3 and has ambitious plans to target revenues of ₹50,000 million in the next five years.

There are many successful regional brands – Himgange herbal products in Uttarakhand, Sakthi Masala in Tamil Nadu, MAPRO Jams and Food Products in Maharashtra and Safed detergent in Kolkata – to name a few. All such regional brands are now delivering on good quality and are successful as they respond faster to consumer preferences.

Interestingly, there are many initiatives being planned by the government of India to improve the infrastructure in rural areas, which will have a salutary effect on increasing the depth and width of the rural markets. One of the focus areas of the government is in the construction of roads and highways. Never before has there been such a massive push towards construction of roads. Unprecedented in terms of speed and scale, this will add road connectivity to large parts of the rural hinterland that have been hitherto isolated. Another major focus area is in rural electrification, where the government is aiming at full electrification of India in the next few years.

In the banking sector as well, there is a quiet revolution unfolding. To get the unbanked population into the banking fold, the Government launched a program called

Jan Dhan Yojana, allowing a person to open a bank account with zero bank balance. This was done to rope in people who did not have a bank account and could not afford to keep a minimum balance in the account. More than 285 million accounts were opened by various banks under this scheme, bringing in the largely unbanked, rural population in the banking fold. With the many new banking licenses issued by the Reserve Bank of India, financial inclusion of rural and unbanked consumers will soon become a reality.

These tectonic changes will have a significant impact on increasing the size of the rural markets, which can only lead to a huge multiplier effect of higher consumption and growth in the size of the market, fuelled by an increase in the movement of goods and services to these areas.

To conclude

What are the takeaways for a marketer wanting to market products in India?

The success of *Sairat* and the other regional products proves that a regional product is an equally good commercial proposition as compared to an expensively mounted national product. With so much diversity, India will continue to have regional brands that will survive and succeed against the might of national and global brands.

Regionalism will have to be an integral part of any marketing strategy for India and marketers need to certainly realign their thinking towards regionalism and plan for regional markets to continue to hold their own on the national or global front. For a national player, the products may have to be localised for a region, which could be done by bringing out small variants or different products for each region. A regional player will have to hold his position by consistently offering a local product of good quality and value, and also looking at markets outside the region.

Rural consumer markets in India are expected to grow faster than their urban counterparts; and regional markets that are so critical in India, will continue to play an important role – *Sairat* just proved this point!

BABA RAMDEV AND THE ART OF BRAND EXTENSION

In India there are thousands of godmen, sadhus, sadhvis, munis and babas. Each of them has their own sect and followers. Traditionally, they have focused on preaching and leading an aesthetic way of life, supported by contributions from their followers. However, a wave of new-age godmen and babas are coming to the fore who are realising that there is commerce to be exploited, beyond their traditional realm of yoga, preaching and religion. Some of the more successful ones are — Baba Ramdev, Sri Sri Ravi Shankar, Saint Dr Gurmeet Ram Rahim Singh Insan and Sadhguru Jaggi Vasudev.

Baba Ramdev's foray in the world of commerce is probably the most successful. Baba is a spiritual leader, best known for popularising yoga. He has a huge following with massive numbers attending his yoga camps in different cities. His programs on the television channel Aastha, are extremely popular and for millions of his followers on social media, Baba Ramdev is truly an iconic yoga guru. However, his tryst with commerce started a decade ago, when farmers from a village near Haridwar mentioned during the conviviality with Baba Ramdev that they were getting rid of their amla (gooseberry) trees because they made no money. Baba promised to buy their amla and started bottling and producing amla juice. The juice was taken to his yoga camps, its benefits propagated, and millions of followers in India and abroad lapped it up. Sales of this juice rocketed!

Around that time, Baba Ramdev founded
Patanjali Ayurved Ltd., to sell ayurvedic
products. He does not own any share in
the company and his close aide Acharya
Balkrishna owns a majority shareholding
and runs the company. Over time, Patanjali
started making other products – hair oil,
soap, cookies, toothpaste and even noodles.
He has recently opened a pure vegetarian
restaurant under the brand name Postik
in Chandigarh and has announced that
Patanjali will soon market desi jeans and
apparel, baby care products, yoga-wear
and shoes. He marches on, increasing his
portfolio of offerings with alacrity. At the pace
at which he is expanding the revenue from
his presently available products and adding
new products, he seems simply unstoppable.

From its humble beginnings, Patanjali has
touched revenues of ₹105,610 million in
2016-17, growing at 111 per cent over
the past year. Their largest selling product
is cow's ghee, with revenues upwards of
₹10,000 million, followed by Dant Kanti
(toothpaste) and Kesh Kanti (hair oil). At this
scorching pace of growth some observers
have predicted that Patanjali revenues are
likely to soon touch ₹200,000 million. Sales
of Patanjali happen through a network of
more than 7,000 Patanjali Chikitsalayas and
Arogya Kendras. This network is expanding
rapidly and they have also tied up with big
retail outlets like Big Bazaar and Reliance
Fresh, resulting in a far greater reach.
With an online presence and sales through
e-commerce sites, Patanjali is also reaching

out to online shoppers. Interestingly, Baba Ramdev is always available to market these products and is omnipresent in its advertising campaigns, on the product and the posters. It has thus become a virtuous cycle – increasing the number of followers feeding into increasing sales of Patanjali products. Truly, an amazing case study of brand extension – from yoga to a portfolio of more than 500 ayurvedic products!

Patanjali is causing a few headaches to established multinational FMCG companies like Hindustan Unilever and Colgate-Palmolive. In fact Baba Ramdev has famously threatened multinationals, saying, "We are hoping to give them a headache. Indians should consume Indian products. Why should we allow multinationals to profit at our expense?"

Other than the brand support of Baba Ramdev, products from Patanjali have a unique proposition – not only do they claim to be of good quality swadeshi products that have health benefits but they are also available at a competitive price. The atta noodles of Patanjali have been priced at ₹15 per packet, against other brands that are priced at ₹25. And to top it all, Baba Ramdev has clearly mentioned that all the profits will be used to support the poor and build schools for the underprivileged. All in all, it is an unbeatable proposition! So what are the strategies of brand extension followed by Baba Ramdev, which have made Patanjali products so successful?

Firstly, he has been immensely successful in mass popularising his core skill – Yoga. His camps in various cities have lakhs of people thronging to learn this ancient science. He has propagated some simple asanas like Kapalbhati – a breathing exercise, which has a salutary effect on a person's health. He has also used the television effectively to beam his programs to those who are unable to physically attend his camps. Focusing on his core strength, he has used the twin strategies of demystifying yoga and reaching out to massive numbers to gain a huge following.

In the corporate sector, management gurus C. K. Prahalad and Gary Hamel introduced the concept of 'core competency' to corporate leaders across the world. Companies like Starbucks, the world's leading retailer of coffee have consistently focused on their core competency of providing high quality beverages and snacks in a clean, well-maintained store and earned a high degree of customer loyalty, almost akin to a cult following.

Secondly, Baba Ramdev has maintained high visibility. He was in the forefront of Anna Hazare's anti-corruption movement in 2011 and has never shied away from airing his political views. He even formed a political party but quickly folded it up before the last general elections and supported Mr. Narendra Modi.

In this age of social media, it is possible to consistently maintain high visibility. Just look at how Sanjeev Kapoor, one of India's most celebrated chefs has adapted to social media. In the pre-Google days, he had hosted a popular television cooking show, Khana Khazana. He has written more than 200 books and runs a 24-hour channel, FoodFood. His website gets more than 8 million unique visitors every month; his Youtube channel has over 1.65 million subscribers and nearly 330 million views. He has 5.5 million followers on Facebook and 1.7 million on Twitter, which is one of the most sought after food handles.

Thirdly, Baba Ramdev has truly understood the art of brand extension and the leveraging of a brand — key components in the concept of brand extension. Celebrity endorsement is not a new concept and it is a multi-billion dollar global business. An interesting example is of Tyra Banks, the famous American model, actor and television personality. In 2014 she successfully launched TYRA Beauty, which has a range of beauty products. She has not just endorsed a brand, but strengthened it by putting her name behind it.

Patanjali is now setting up factories across India to enhance its reach, increasing its network and also expanding its portfolio — all in all, Patanjali is on a roll! Who could have imagined that a spiritual leader would extend his brand and build a huge business? Who would have thought that a yogi would endorse a brand of noodles? Baba Ramdev has proved that if good quality products are made available, brand extension can indeed become successful.

Another godman who entered the FMCG market is Saint Dr Gurmeet Ram Rahim Singh Insan, who sold the products under the brand name of MSG. Gurmeet Ram Rahim Singh was the spiritual leader and the head of the socio-spiritual organisation, Dera Sacha Sauda (DSS), which was founded in 1948. Headquartered in Sirsa Haryana, DSS claims to have a massive following of 50 million people in India and across the globe. As part of its social programs, DSS organises events like blood donation drives, tree planting etc. It also has many Limca Book records and Guinness Book records, including a bizarre Guinness Book record of the most people tossing coins simultaneously on 15 August 2011.

In August 2017, he was convicted of raping two women, sentenced to 20 years in prison and is now lodged in a jail in Rohtak. After his arrest, there were many incidents of arson and the DSS got a lot of negative publicity. Prior to his conviction, he enjoyed tremendous clout and all political parties would woo him before any significant elections.

Unlike other godmen, Gurmeet Ram Rahim Singh had followed the Bollywood route to propagate his message. His first film was released in February 2015 and his latest film *Jattu Engineer* on 19 May 2017. Despite poor reviews, it is claimed that the gross collection of each of these movies exceeds ₹1,000 million. Irrespective of the economics, it is an interesting example of the way a spiritual leader had used a popular medium like Bollywood to popularise, propagate and reach out to his followers. In fact, much before he produced and acted in movies, he had started composing and singing songs and releasing albums. He has churned out six albums so far and has held more than 100 rock shows and the Dera claims that more than 100,000 followers attend each of these shows.

In April 2016 Gurmeet Ram Rahim Singh launched his MSG range of 'swadeshi and organic products' at the headquarters of the Dera in Sirsa. There were more than 150 products under the MSG brand covering a wide range from rice, pickles and honey to bottled water and noodles. Gurmeet Ram Rahim Singh appeared in advertisements which promoted his MSG products. With his conviction, sales of MSG products plummeted and it shows the risk run by godmen in promoting commercial products which are closely identified with them. However, if DSS appoints a new leader and the leader pursues this path of hawking products, it can still succeed, due to the inherent advantages which the Dera enjoys.

Firstly, DSS has millions of followers. DSS is an old organisation, having been founded in 1948. Its followers are a captive market and will lap up anything that the leader propagates. In the corporate sector, Apple has massive numbers of 'cult-like' followers who lap up innovative products from the company, year after year.

Secondly, the Dera has 46 ashrams across the country. Initially confined to the Punjab-Haryana area, it has spread across India and also has branches abroad including the USA and Canada. These ashrams and branches provide a good network for purveying MSG products to the followers. A large network of outlets in a large country like India is clearly a big advantage and many companies like Starbucks, Domino's and CCD are furiously expanding their network to increase their reach and purvey their products.

With the conviction of Ram Rahim, sales of MSG products have nose-dived. Can the organisation recover from the shock of the conviction of its leader? Will it appoint a new leader? Will the new leader pursue the path of aggressively pushing commercial products? Despite the present crisis, the Dera has an opportunity to revive its sales if it alacritously appoints a successor who pursues this path of commercial products.

Yet another successful spiritual leader is Sri Sri Ravi Shankar who has become a global phenomenon with his popular Art of Living course and Sudarshan Kriya.

Born in 1956, Ravi Shankar was a gifted child and is believed to have been able to recite parts of the Bhagavad Gita at the age of four. In 1982, he entered a 10-day period of silence in Shimoga, in the state of Karnataka. He held his first program in Shimoga and this event was the starting point of his transition from Ravi Shankar to

Sri Sri Ravi Shankar. Sri Sri established his Art of Living (AOL) foundation soon thereafter. At the centre of his course is the practice of 'Sudarshan Kriya', a form of meditation and a series of cyclical breathing exercises. To celebrate 35 years of AOL, Sri Sri organised the World Cultural Festival on the banks of the Yamuna river in March 2016. Held over three days, the event was attended by a galaxy of luminaries including the Prime Minister of India. The organisers claimed that the festival attracted more than 3.75 million visitors from 155 countries. Sri Sri has now built a global empire with his Art of Living courses and claims to have touched the lives of more than 300 million people across the world through his teachings and courses – truly, an astounding number!

Sri Sri started selling his products in 2003 under the umbrella of Sri Sri Ayurveda (SSA) Trust, the FMCG arm of AOL Foundation. Under the Sri Sri brand, there is a portfolio of products including ayurvedic energisers, medicines, juices, herbal teas, creams, toothpastes, shampoos, body care lotions, scrubs, soaps, cleansing milks, and anti-diabetic tablets. These products are sold through 600 franchise stores called Divine Stores, which are set up by his followers. They are also available online on e-commerce sites.

Probably, the success of Patanjali has motivated the Sri Sri Ayurveda Trust to plan an expansion of their portfolio of offerings to include breakfast cereals, cookies, edible oil and ready-to-cook items. They are also expanding their coverage by opening 2,500 stores across India. Given the massive global popularity and following of Sri Sri, there is deep potential to market products under his brand. Baba Ramdev may have been far more aggressive in his sales and marketing strategies and notched faster growth, but products of Sri Sri will be lurking behind.

If you need to find out the most popular spiritual guru with the corporate czars, the answer is simple: it is Sadhguru Jaggi Vasudev. Sadhguru is the best-selling author of *Inner Engineering: A Yogi's Guide to Joy,* which entered the Washington Post and the New York Times bestseller list in multiple categories. Besides this book, Jaggi Vasudev has authored numerous other books. A consummate showman, he is immensely popular with the corporate world. He supports their causes and propagates the thought that business is necessary for nation building. He has assiduously built an empire which has 150 branches across the globe and has touched more than two million people with his Inner Engineering programme.

Born in 1957 in Mysore (Karnataka), Jagadish or Jaggi developed an interest in nature at a young age. After graduating in literature from Mysore University, he became an entrepreneur and had a successful run with businesses in poultry farming, real estate and construction. With this material comfort, Jaggi decided to travel around the country. His moment of enlightenment came in 1982, at the young age of twenty-five. While sitting on the Chamundi Hills outside of Bengaluru, he felt a deep spiritual experience. For more than a year after that, he travelled extensively on his motorcycle and practised yoga. In 1983, he conducted his first yoga class in Mysore with a handful of participants. He lived off the money made from his business and did not charge any money to the people attending his yoga class. Whatever money was paid by them was donated to local charity. Over the years, his yoga programmes became popular and he finally set up his Isha Yoga Centre in 1994, near the Velliangiri Hills close to Coimbatore.

He founded the Isha Foundation, a non-profit, non-religious organisation, entirely run by volunteers. It regularly holds programmes for self-awareness of Isha Yoga, which the Sadhguru claims is a comprehensive system that integrates the core of yogic science and which springs from methods disseminated over 15,000 years ago. The Inner Engineering programme introduces people to the practice of meditation and pranayam. Jaggi Vasudev also holds regular classes for corporates leaders to teach them Isha Yoga and his version of 'inclusive economics' which encourages them to inculcate a sense of compassion and inclusiveness in their business.

In 2011, Sadhguru launched Isha Arogya under the aegis of the Isha Foundation. Isha Arogya claims to be a comprehensive approach to health, representing a paradigm shift in wellness and health, with holistic therapies for ailments. It also offers massages, nutritional supplements, yoga programmes and rejuvenating therapies. At the same time Isha Herbal was launched with five products initially. From this initial launch, the product range has rapidly expanded to include energy drinks, honey, instant mixes, healthy snacks, pickles, instant drinks, yoga accessories, clothing, fragrances, jewellery, body care, art and craft, home décor, furniture and kitchenware. These products are sold through Isha's own stores and are also available online on their site, the app and through e-commerce companies.

These products may not have become a raging success like the Patanjali products, but have the potential to grow. Unlike the Patanjali model, Isha products have not been marketed heavily. The Sadhguru has a large and loyal following and the volume of sales is bound to grow. Known to be aesthetic, his product range is rather different from the range of products offered by the others. Items like furniture, jewellery and home décor are certainly not produced by the other godmen. This differentiation and his steadily increasing following will surely have an impact in the long run.

To conclude

India is probably the largest laboratory for brand extension by godmen and spiritual leaders. Truly pioneering and unprecedented, these leaders have launched some products which are quite distanced from their core competency. These are lapped up by followers and are increasingly consumed by non-followers too, based on WOM (Word of Mouth) publicity, creating a huge domino effect.

In times to come, we will probably see two major trends.

One, any godman with a decent following will launch products and urge his followers to consume them. With the large number of godmen in India, we will see many more products, which will push the traditional, large FMCG companies to the wall. These companies will respond by launching their own version of natural or ayurvedic products or may even collaborate with a godman for endorsement. In the toothpaste segment, Patanjali's Dant Kanti toothpaste garnered a market share of three percent in 2016, double its market share in the earlier year. Colgate-Palmolive has responded by launching Colgate Herbal toothpaste. More importantly, the huge marketing by Patanjali has built awareness for the 'natural' segment and Dabur Babool toothpaste has seen a growth too. Patanjali will need to hone its strategies to ensure that it captures the maximum market share of market creation for the 'natural' segment. A nightmare situation for them would be where they create the market and other companies capture it by their own products in this segment!

Two, the larger companies (like Patanjali) will start pushing their products in the global markets. They will initially target their own followers and after that, overseas Indians yearning to consume a slice of India. The more difficult step would be to target non-Indian global consumers. If the product positioning is done effectively, it is possible to succeed in this market as well, since global consumers are increasingly looking at 'natural' markets.

Is there anything which can potentially spoil the party? As the downfall of Ram Rahim has shown, the one huge risk is that the products are too closely associated with the brand of an individual. Should there be any significant dent in the image of the godman that garners negative publicity, the revenues will take an immediate dip. But as Baba Ramdev has shown, it is possible to be truly successful in brand extension. For Baba and his ilk, the party has just begun – or, to put it differently, this is just the first asana in the yoga session!